Praise for Get a Job Without Going Crazy...

"Every job seeker MUST read *How to Get a Job Without Going Crazy*. Donna's clear and straightforward strategy will help you develop your story, write a compelling resume, give a strong interview, and conduct a successful search. She blends this common sense approach with insider knowledge of what goes through the minds of HR professionals and hiring managers – and shares the scoop on how and what they do to fill their openings with the best candidate. Read this book to discover the strategy and insights to land the job that's right for you!"

- Dan Clemens, Business Coach and Author
A Perfect Season: A Coach's Journey to Learning, Competing, and Having Fun in Youth Baseball

"Death and Taxes are absolutes, but many of us miss the third of the trilogy . . . Change. Ms. Shannon has written a thorough guide that provides you with choices for a clear, concise plan and pathway through the many changes that may seem overwhelming in today's marketplace. Read it, study it, internalize it, use it . . . and Go get it! I did."

- Gary Warstler, Estate Manager

"A great over-all tool job seekers need for their tool box to land that 'Dream Job.' This book covers all aspects of getting your resume past the HR department and into the hiring manager's hands. This practical guide is easy to read and to use to put together your resume, cover letters and interview assistance. A must-have tool for your toolbox."

- Wendy Purcell, Medical Administration

"Ms. Shannon's book is direct, informative and entertaining. It presents the truths and myths of effective self-marketing. Her HR experience and expertise make her insightful, practical book a must read for those looking to compete in today's job market."

- W. Williamson, Executive Luxury Lifestyle Management

"Definitely a well thought-out approach to 'what to do next' when faced with either finding the right job or for finding your NEXT perfect job if you've been laid off."

Elaine Miller, AITP
Former National President of   ology Professionals

D1010039

DONNA L. SHANNON

HOW TO
GET A JOB
WITHOUT
GOING *CRAZY*

2ND EDITION

A PRACTICAL GUIDE TO YOUR EMPLOYMENT SEARCH

Donna L. Shannon
The Personal Touch Career Services
1425 Brentwood St, Suite 11
Lakewood, CO 80214

www.personaltouchcareerservices.com
info@personaltouchcareerservices.com

For Ryan
Who puts up with my insanity

Table of Contents

Listing of Illustrations and Samples

Chapter 2 - Your Goals
Figure 2.1: Define your goals

Chapter 3 - The Key Element Detector™

Figure 3.1: Blank Key Element Detector™
Figure 3.2: Sample job postings
Figure 3.3: Completed Key Element Detector™
Figure 3.4: Sample Resume based on the Key Element Detector™

Chapter 4 - Resumes
Figure 4.1: Hidden information on a resume
Figure 4.2: A simple formatting trick
Figure 4.3: Anatomy of a resume
Figure 4.4: How to list additional experience
Figure 4.5: The Laundry List resume
Figure 4.6: Text conversion for a Laundry List resume
Figure 4.7: Traps for a Laundry List resume
Figure 4.8: The Paragraph resume
Figure 4.9: Text conversion for a Paragraph resume
Figure 4.10: Traps for a Paragraph resume
Figure 4.11: The Outline resume
Figure 4.12: Text conversion for an Outline resume
Figure 4.13: Traps for Outline resumes
Figure 4.14: The Functional resume
Figure 4.15: Problems with computer templates
Figure 4.16: Problems with tab formatting
Figure 4.17: The Creative resume

Chapter 5 - Resume Writing
Figure 5.1: The Passion Statement formula
Figure 5.2: Revising wordy resumes
Figure 5.3: The dangers of falling in love (with your resume)
Figure 5.4: Expanding thin resumes
Figure 5.5: Adding details that matter

Chapter 11 - Interview Tips

Chapter 1 - What Really Happens in the HR Department

In the quiet Human Resources department, a lone figure works at her desk. Poring over the stack of resumes, the director hopes to find that perfect candidate, the one who not only meets every criterion, but also has the "spark." She sighs as she lifts the next packet off the paper mountain. She reads carefully, weighing the merits of each candidate before setting their resume aside. Her tired eyes fall on the next cover letter, low expectations written all over her face.

Her pulse quickens as she reads with disbelief – this could be the one! The experience sketched out in the letter is a perfect match for the company's needs. Eagerly, she flips to the resume: it is a home run! The perfect skill set, the perfect background, the perfect degree. She can't wait another moment to talk to this candidate. She must snatch him up before another company does.

Her hands fly to the phone. She dials nervously – what if he's not there? What if he's interviewing somewhere else right now? She draws a tight breath while the phone rings once, then twice... Her heart skips a beat as you answer the phone. Now it is only a matter of going through the formalities of the interview before they can offer you the job of your dreams.

* * *

Did you enjoy that? Good. Because that is never going to happen. Now that the fantasy is over with, we can uncover the nasty truth about what the Human Resources (HR) department is really like.

The truth is that most HR departments receive a deluge of candidates every day, far more than they could ever hope to read with any great depth or understanding. In order to process the mountain of resumes, every single company - big or small - will create simple tricks to screen candidates. You have probably heard some of these already, such as "the resume will only be read for 30 seconds." Many of these rumors are true, but it is important to understand *why* in order to get through the system.

So like it or not, here is what a real HR department is like:

HR departments reduce the candidate field by up to 90% - or more - before forwarding the top candidates to the hiring managers
The HR department is not your buddy, looking for the perfect job for you; they are c looking for ways to CUT YOU. The survivors of this ordeal are considered as the top candidates. However, because of the screening process, these people might not be the *most qualified* candidates.

If you don't want to be a qualified casualty, learn the screening process.

The average amount of time spent reading a resume the first time is 30 seconds, and not everyone gets a second read
HR professionals do not spend time pouring over the details in your resume. They are taking a quick look to see if you have the minimum skills and/or experience they want. If HR can't see your value in 30 seconds or less, your resume is rejected.

Very few people are excited about reading through a stack of resumes. And who can blame them? Most resumes are boring, monotonous, poorly written, or filled with bragging. That's why...

Lower-level HR employees do the initial screening
It is tedious going through a stack of resumes. So they make the assistants do the first layer of cuts. Or worse, they are let a computer do the screening. Either way, these screeners follow very literal and specific instructions. If your resume is not using the right key terms or jargon, you probably will be cut, no matter how qualified you are. Not only that, the screeners have very little oversight on their work. Nobody is checking to see if you got cut or not - unless you are networking with managers at the company.

HR departments and hiring managers won't read everything you send them
This fact is often a shock for many job seekers. One common misconception is that a strong cover letter can overcome a weak resume, or vice versa. However, that is not how screeners read the submitted material.

2

The common practice is to read the resume first. Then, if it is interesting enough, they read your cover letter. On the other hand, they may not understand why you applied at all. They hope your cover letter will add some insight. In either case, your cover letter and even your references need to support your resume, not the other way around. That means your resume really needs to stand out from the competition.

Job descriptions are not absolutes
Ever hear the statement; "if you don't have all of the qualifications, apply anyway?" That is true! Hiring managers and HR professionals do not spend hours constructing the perfect job description. They throw it together quickly and according to the company's approved format.

Whether the job description is dead-on or just an approximation, it is still used as a tool to cut candidates. However, here's the tricky part: some things are added to deter lower-level candidates. The hiring manager may not care about these standards at all. HR departments are famous for adding requirements because it follows the company's format.

Don't let a misguided HR screener control your entire fate. Reaching the hiring manager can actually save you from a mistaken cut - if you handle it the right way.

Employers won't hire the perfect candidate. They hire the closest match at the right price
The right price does not mean the cheapest candidate. They are looking for someone who matches the most critical skills and experience while staying within a given budget.

* * *

Basic Rules for Surviving the HR Department
With all of this working against you, the job search may seem more difficult than ever. However, once you understand the rules, you can make them work for you - and know when to break them.

In the upcoming chapters, we'll cover the specific techniques to get past the guard dogs. In essence, they all boil down to the biggest unspoken rules:

Three Rules for Dealing with HR:

1. **Don't let them assume**

2. **Don't be annoying**

3. **Don't create extra work**

Never let the employers assume *anything*
Anytime the HR department has to assume anything, they will always assume against you. This also includes *mistakes THEY make,* such as adding up your years of experience.

Be absolutely clear and concise on your resume. This is true for dates, skill sets, past employers, past responsibilities, degrees, and even your amount of experience. Your survival depends on how well you can convey critical information.

Don't be annoying – on paper, on the phone or in person
Many people do not know proper etiquette, especially when it comes to formal business correspondence like a cover letter. It can be as simple as taking an overly familiar tone in emails or not using professional language. Professional doesn't mean stuffy, but it needs to be genuine, respectful and direct.

Contrary to popular belief, it is acceptable to call the HR department IF you have a legitimate reason. However, calling up and asking for an interview is very annoying. Doing it in person without an appointment is even worse. Being dismissive or rude to anyone at the company is very dangerous. Getting attention is fine, but in the employment game, negative attention is the sure-fire trip to the rejection pile. If you annoy anybody too much - including everyone from the receptionist to the hiring managers - they will find an excuse to cut you.

Don't create extra work

The more thinking HR has to do, the more work it creates. That is bad news for you. To combat this apathy, you need to be absolutely clear.

Tell them exactly which job you want: don't expect the HR department to figure it out. If you are applying for more than one position at a company, send in two resumes, with a customized cover letter for each. Anything that promotes communication while saving time is your best tool. Use direct and specific language so they can appreciate your qualifications immediately.

Learn the rules of the game

Companies want to hire confident, capable employees. How do they determine this? By how well you navigate their hiring maze. There *are* universal recruiting techniques that employers use. You need to know them - your survival depends on it.

Chapter 2 - How Your Goals Affect Your Strategy

When it comes to setting a goal for their job search, most people think in terms of target jobs or target employers. In fact, if you don't have at least an idea of what kind of jobs you want or potential employers, it can be very challenging to find a job at all.

Without a vision of your target job, you cannot attain it. A lot depends on knowing your industry, job title, company size and even the experience level. Unfortunately, many job seekers start with a clear vision of their target job, but as the search grinds on, an edge of desperation enters into their strategy. Rather than researching specific employers, their cry becomes "I'll do anything!" When widening the net to jobs far under their experience level or on the fringe of their target industries fails to generate job leads, depression sets in.

The truth is that once you have lost your focus, you have lost the employers' interest. Employers don't want to hire someone who will do anything. They have a specific need to fill and are looking for a proper match. It is impossible to show an excellent match for a target job if the resume is crafted to highlight "versatility." Remember, HR departments won't read a resume with the mindset of seeing how they can use you; they want to cut you.

You can pursue different career options, such as sales, public relations and customer service. However, each target job requires a separate resume and different job searching tactics. Understanding this from the beginning helps develop your strategies.

Take five minutes and write down all the different target jobs that fit with your career plans. Don't be critical or make judgments; consider all possibilities. In the upcoming chapters, we will cut this list down by taking an analytical view of the real requirements for these positions, but you need a sizable list to start with:

My target jobs:

Figure 2.1: Define your goals

What I'm Willing to Do	What I'm NOT Willing to do

COMPENSATION

Salary is a touchy issue. Many people aren't comfortable with talking about the hard numbers with other people. Get over it. In modern job searching, you must be up front with your salary requirements. That means you need to know your bottom line. How much do you need? How much are you worth? And how much will the market bear?

You salary range can be expressed as a dollar amount, such as $70,000 to 80,000 a year. It is best to work with a range, rather than an exact number. When you contact HR departments and hiring managers, you will always be talking in terms of range until you get to the job offer.

In some cases, you may need to take less salary. If you are completely changing your industry or career, expect to take a hit. If you are considering taking less money, make sure you know how much you can afford. Crunch some numbers to make sure it will work for you. In other words, create a realistic budget with several different scenarios, both for increasing and decreasing salary expectations.

A Great Truth

Never take a job that pays less than you can afford just because they promise you a raise later. Raises are a percentage of your current salary. If you start too low, the increase will be too low as well. Most job seekers change jobs to get a 7% increase in salary. The average raise is 3-5%. It is possible to land a job with a 20% salary increase - you just have to maneuver the hiring maze correctly.

Keep your salary requirements realistic

Do some research on salary ranges in your area. Plenty of websites list useful and current salary statistics. For example, http://www.salary.com will tell you the salary ranges within your own ZIP code, based on job descriptions and experience levels. (You don't have to pay to get this information, although any website like this wants to sell you a package.) Armed with the average salaries in your area, you can create a realistic expectation. http://www.Glassdoor.com is another free site, where former and current employees can share their salary ranges in confidence. Be careful with this source; many contributors are bitter employees, so take everything with a grain of salt. If you are considering different types of jobs, be sure to conduct research on salary expectations for each job.

Compensation is more than just a paycheck. Considerations such as vacation accrual, sick time, benefits and retirement packages add real value to any job. What benefits are absolute requirements? Which ones would be nice to have? Don't forget the fringe benefits, such as paid parking, cell phones, company car... and the most important one of all - do they provide free coffee?

LOCATION

How far do you want to commute in the morning? Are you flexible for the right opportunity? Do you want to travel as part of your job, and if so, how much? Is there a specific area of the city you would prefer, or one you would not consider under any circumstances? If you are looking to relocate, your job searching methods will change drastically.

Location includes more than just where the workplace is. Think about the actual building itself. Does a steel and glass box seem too sterile? Or a converted house too casual? Do you need a window and sunlight, or is a more enclosed area acceptable? Do you need your own office, or can you handle working in a cubicle? Interior design can be an issue as well; how important is your environment to your mental state? Think about noise: does a lot of noise drive you crazy? Or is it the silence that grates on you? How about exposure to the public?

Your lifestyle influences work locations as well. Do you need to be close to your children's schools or activities? If you are considering going to school yourself, what colleges are in the area? Do you want to work close to shopping areas, restaurants or parks you can visit over your lunch hour?

Relocation changes job search tactics drastically. Few employers help with relocation costs anymore, and fewer still will consider interviewing someone outside of their area. Are you willing to move before you have a job? Be sure to research all of the financial factors in a new city, including housing costs, cost of living and relative salary ranges.

INDUSTRY

Be very realistic about your industry's direction. This is a time of flux. Many traditional industries have to evolve or die - just look at the fate of newspapers vs. the internet. Can you anticipate the future growth or shrinkage of your sector? What worked in the past may need a new approach. Seek innovation in your own career search.

If you are thinking of a career in a distressed industry, you need to weigh your options carefully. Finding another job in challenged market will take a long time, simply because so many candidates are competing for fewer positions. You might want to consider of other industries that appeal to you. On the other hand, some industries are thriving in this changing economy. Researching statistical data available online or at the library can show trends in terms of revenue, industry growth and historical performance.

Remember that new industries can be very volatile. Start-up companies are more vulnerable and may not last. However, if they make it, the rewards can be huge. Likewise, some industries are being phased out because of our cultural changes. For example, retailers need to try new tactics to drive customers into the store to compete with online sales. Traditional broadcast radio stations are losing audiences to MP3 players, smart phones, satellite sources and internet radios. If you can anticipate market trends, you are a very desirable candidate.

If you are changing industries, gaining education could be a factor. Are you willing to go to school and invest in your own training? Fewer employers are offering tuition reimbursement, especially when so many educated candidates are available.

Government influence matters, especially if the industry itself is highly regulated. Private employers who work as government contractors must follow specific guidelines in their hiring procedures. If you want to be a civil servant yourself, your job search tactics change dramatically. It could take three to four months to get an interview after submitting a resume. Government resumes are vastly different from normal business resumes as well: no other sector will require such comprehensive documents.

Nonprofits have their own unique challenges. Since the economic downturn, many charities are struggling to stay afloat. If you are drawn to a non-profit organization, make sure that it is a cause that receives plenty of public support.

COMPANY CULTURE

Company culture extends beyond whether it is a casual work environment. Culture includes the size of the company, longevity, future opportunities, environment and, of course, the managers. Think about past jobs. What environment did you thrive in? Which one felt like professional suffocation?

Business size has a huge impact on both the culture and the hiring tactics. Small companies tend to ask for more varied responsibilities from their employees. It is easier to reach hiring managers. However, small businesses will fill their openings quicker. By contrast, a large company will use more rigid job descriptions and a more complex hiring procedure.

Think about how you want your day to be structured. Are you a "9 to 5er," thriving in an office environment? Or would you want flexible hours? Are you open to overtime or working longer hours, either with or without the overtime pay? Would working in an office suck the life out of you? How about working in the evenings, or on weekends?

One culture aspect people tend to gloss over is the introvert/ extrovert aspect. Do you find outgoing people annoying? Do you find it difficult to pay attention to the introverted boss? Highly social team-oriented atmosphere or working alone - which situation drives you crazy? If you enjoy working on teams, what role do you want to be in: the leader, the supporter, the contributor or the glue that holds everything together?

Are there specific personality types you want to avoid? Most people say "micro-manager" or "control freak" right about now... but if you do not clearly define this now and ask questions about culture in the interview, you may walk into this situation blind.

Increasingly, employers are hiring contract and part-time employees. Is self-directed employment a possibility for you? How does this change your salary expectations? If you are considering contract work, remember to add in enough to cover your taxes and expenses.

RESPONSIBILITY

Are you just starting on your professional path, willing to make it your primary focus in your life? Are you willing to put in the extra hours to

13

get noticed on the promotion track? On the other hand, are other factors becoming more important, such as leisure time, family time or a chance to travel the world? Or are you are you looking forward to retiring in a few years?

Where do you want to be in the next five years? No, this is not the cheesy interview question - be honest about what you want to do. Career planning is necessary, especially in a challenging economy. If you do not take the time to plot out your path, you will not find your way.

Even in rough times, consider the next job's impact on your overall career. Sometimes a step back is necessary to move forward. While you are pursuing your main career, you may have a "fall back" job as well. A lower-level job may not be ideal; however, it may be necessary for the paycheck. Considering a lower job dictates its' own strategy. Just because you're willing to take less doesn't mean the employer is going to believe you. The challenge with landing a lower-level job is convincing the employers that you want it. You must face and overcome these objections.

How much real responsibility do you want? Do you want to work individually, or as part of a group? Would you want to be responsible for the outcome? Or would you prefer to be the support person? Do you want to manage others? What personalities do you find difficult to manage?

MY DREAM JOB
Take a few moments and think about what your absolute dream job would be. What do you see yourself doing all day? What tasks do you like best? Is it all one thing, or is a mix?

When all things are considered, what really makes you happy?

My ideal title and responsibilities:

_____

My ideal salary situation:

_____

My ideal location:

_____

I see my industry evolving into:

_____

I can take advantage of this by:

_____

I love working with this kind of company:

_____

I am willing to try:

_____

My best days are arranged like this:

_____

I am committed to:

_____

Final words on your goals

Your goals will shape your job search. For example, small companies will use more economical job postings than a large corporation. By understanding this, you can develop a job search strategy.

The same is true with different target jobs. What might be a great tactic for a marketing position may not work for a pure management role. To be effective, you will need to create different resumes for each type of job.

Stick to your goals even when the going gets tough. Employers want to hire confident candidates. If you know what you want in specific terms, you come across as a confident future employee.

Chapter 3 - Your Secret Weapon: The Key Element Detector™

When most people get ready to write their resume, they sit down and try to think about what was important about their last job. This is a critical mistake; it doesn't matter what you think was important, but what the HR departments and hiring mangers think is important. But how can you figure that out? This is where the Key Element Detector™ comes into play.

Why Key Words Are Important

First and foremost, you need to know why key words, phrases and experience are so important. Every single HR department will use key words to screen resumes, to some degree. HR people don't have time to read your resume; they are scanning it for the key words or phrases.

In bigger companies, this can be even more important, as they may rely on a computer program to do the initial level of screening. In that case, the computer only reacts to *the exact words* and will not recognize phrases with similar meaning. For example, if the job description reads "proficient in Word" and you write "proficient in Microsoft Office," you could get screened out because the computer was not programmed to recognize that Word is part of MS Office.

Silly, huh?

But that is the way HR works.

Even when an actual human being is doing the screening, he or she may not recognize similar terms. Technical positions, such as IT or graphic design, run into this problem quite a bit. An entry-level HR screener just doesn't have the experience to recognize that Photoshop and InDesign are similar programs. If you can get your resume to the hiring manager, there is a better chance that he or she will understand the comparable skills - but you still have to navigate the HR maze at the same time.

Key words are also important for the passive job search. Basically, if you are ever contacted directly from a recruiter, you are considered a *passive candidate.* Passive candidates are people who did not actively apply for the job on their own. More and more frequently, recruiters are seeking candidates on websites like LinkedIn.com, especially for management, technical jobs, marketing, sales and niche industries. Some employers will also use the resume data bases from a major employment sites, such as Monster.com or CareerBuilder.com. No matter what website they are using, the key words are the only way the recruiters can find passive candidates.

A Great Truth

What works on HR will work on the hiring manager, but for different reasons.

Simple tricks to get past the screener make your entire presentation look more professional and relevant. Why? Because you are literally speaking their language. Every industry and every position has its own associated jargon – the specific words people in that professional culture use to describe something.

Some resume experts will try to convince you that jargon has no place on a modern resume. However, that is not true - proper use of jargon is how a recruiter or hiring manager knows that you understand the industry. In one of my past positions, I was recruiting some technical engineering positions for a biodiesel company. Specifically, if the candidate properly used the word "transesterfication" in his resume or LinkedIn profile, I knew that they were a viable candidate. (Transesterfication, by the way, is the chemical process that turns animal fats or vegetable oils into biodiesel fuel.)

So if key words are so important, how do you know what the right key words are?

The Key Element Detector™

The Key Element Detector™ is a process of analyzing a number of different job descriptions to determine what are the universal requirements and experience for any job. It is designed to identify what really matters for each and every type of job... no matter what the field or experience level.

To make it work correctly, you need to analyze a respectable sample of current job descriptions for your targeted job.

IMPORTANT NOTE: only work on *one* job title at a time. If you are interested in several types of positions, such as Office Manager, Administrative Assistant and Executive Assistant, do a separate Key Element Detector™ for each one. By using a large sample set, you will discover the universal requirements for this job. Look at jobs on various websites, such as monster.com or careerbuilder.com. These don't have to be your dream job or dream company. What you are gunning for are detailed job descriptions.

Steps for the Key Element Detector:

    1. Research the job

    2. Analyze the data

    3. Continue the process for each job description

    4. Compare the results

---

1.   Research the job

Pull up and print several detailed job postings or descriptions from the internet for the specific position. Choose at least five to ten. The more, the better. If you do not have enough job descriptions, your results will be skewed.

2.   Analyze the data

Starting with the first job description, list the specific criteria for each job description on the left, and the specific duties on the right. For hard skills – ones that can be tested, such as computer abilities – be sure to list details such as the specific program names. Don't forget to include the soft skills, such as "attention to detail" or "team player."

Remember to include years of experience, proficiency or education levels requested in the ad.

3.   Continue process for each job description

Go on to the next job ad. For criteria or duties that are repeated, put a check mark next to it. If new skills or duties are listed, write them down on your Key Element Detector™ (see Figure 1 for a blank template). Repeat for each job ad.

4.   Compare results with your abilities

These are the talents, skills, experience and education you need to highlight in your resume.

Figure 3.1 Blank Key Element Detector™

Repetition	Criteria / Requirements	Duties	Repetition

Understanding the results

Skills and duties with more check marks are the critical key elements for the job. When crafting your resume, you must show these key elements or else you won't get past the screening process. Even if you do get through the screening, the hiring manager won't see how you fit his needs.

Pay attention to the focus of these ads. Are a number of different of skills listed? Or are they looking for specific experience levels? Is there more emphasis on soft skills, such as communication or people skills? Look at the bigger picture - it's not just about key words, but the overall package.

Big Tip: Years of experience

Very few people mention how many years of experience they have when writing a resume. Job seekers assume the HR department will take the time to add up, based on the dates listed on the resume. They might do that – if they were interested enough to take the time. Remember, any time you let them assume, it will always work against you. Not only that, but you also run the risk that they may add your years incorrectly.

As a resume writer, I constantly add a mention of years of experience to the skill set. When you provide the actual years as a numerical value, you can easily advance to the next level in the screening process. Plus, the years are mapped out for the hiring manager as well. This is another quick way to make an impact on the right people in the shortest reading time possible.

A very effective technique is putting the years in terms of "2+." This tactic keeps the resume relevant without forcing you to update it constantly. An additional benefit is managing the age factor. If I am uncomfortable with a potential employer guessing my age, writing "number+" years experience on the resume is still accurate - even if you experience is 10 years, and they only want 5. Tailoring the years of experience to what they request in the job description also reduces the risk of being cut as "overqualified."

What about accomplishments?

Sometimes employers are looking for results and past accomplishments. If you run across statements like "demonstrated ability to" or "proven track record" this means they are looking for accomplishments or accolades in your resume.

One big trend in resume writing is the use of past accomplishments, to the point where any mention of skills is sacrificed. This is a valid approach – for some jobs. Sales and management jobs always have an emphasis on results, because that is the critical key element for that type of job. By comparison, the most desired feature of an executive assistant is experience plus expertise across a large skill set. An IT person's biggest selling points are the multitude of systems they know how to use and their various certifications.

Highlighted accomplishments can serve you well, but choose examples that support the overall valued key elements of the job. Reducing costs, increasing productivity, increasing sales, streamlining processes and upholding standards are all important to employers, especially if these qualities directly relate to the employer's unspoken needs.

Trouble finding your accomplishments?

It is important to note your performance level in your resume. Don't let them assume what you did because you held a certain job title. Just because it is clear to you doesn't mean that it is clear to the reader. When you define the job by scope, HR gets a better concept of your work. Scope tells them the workload volume, size of projects, numbers of clients, and so on. Scope shows the intensity of your work, giving a clear picture of your capacities. It is always expressed in quantifiable terms. For example, "managing a team of 20 sales representatives" is a lot more informative than "Responsible for managing the sales team."

The value of this tool

I am not an expert in all fields, but I am an expert in resume writing. I always start a client's resume with a Key Element Detector™. Without it, I am just as liable to fall for my own assumptions.

For example, a past client of mine was looking for a nursing position. Her lack of interviews didn't make sense. This is a high demand industry and she certainly had the right skill set and experience. I asked her to bring in the printed job ads, and we worked through the Key Element Detector™ together. What we discovered was she had transposed the letters in her certifications; from ACLS certification to ALCS. When we corrected this error and wrote her resume to reflect the universal key elements of the job, she began to get interviews the next week.

Many times people don't realize the importance of what they do every day, especially when it comes to resume writing. What you think is most important may vary greatly from the general view in the employment scene. Using the Key Element Detector™ takes the guesswork out.

But what about those clichés?

Some people are in a full-out revolt about the clichés that plague resumes: "detail-oriented", "results-oriented" and of course the classic "excellent oral and written communication skills." Why in the world would you put these worn-out phrases in the resume?

Unfortunately, you do have to use these terms - *if they consistently turn up in your Key Element Detector™*. HR is still screening by these phrases, which means you have to use them.

Missing elements

One of the really great benefits of using the Key Element Detector™ is that it allows you to discover the missing pieces. For example, if a particular computer program you are not skilled with comes up over and over again, go take a class to fill in that hole in your abilities.

A Great Truth

Education is always important, even if the degree wasn't completed or was in another field. However, possessing all of the desired skills and experience can be more important that a degree - depending on the industry.

In some careers, not having the right degree can be a deal breaker. However, once again, it depends on the industry. Going through a Key Element Detector™ is an ideal way to determine how important a degree is. If all the employers are asking for is some

Second sample advertisement

Administrative Assistant

We are seeking a sharp individual who can work in a small office environment supporting the executive director and office administrator. This individual must have strong written and oral communication skills coupled with excellent customer service skills to support the organization's 3,300 members via phone and email. You will maintain a database of members, produce and distribute publications, products and materials in printed format, electronic, DVD, CD Rom formats and answer the phones. You must be computer savvy in all Microsoft applications. A business background is preferred with strict attention to details a must!

Requirements & Experience

- Minimum 3 years experience working in an office environment
- Prefer 1 to 2 years of college or business school
- Strong work ethic, dependable, reliable, detail oriented a must
- Ability to work in a small team office environment
- Able to travel on a limited basis, approximately 1 week per quarter.

Skills

- Excellent communication skills, especially in English composition
- Intermediate level skills and experienced with Microsoft Office; Word, Excel, Outlook, and Power Point

Third sample advertisement

Administrative Assistant
Junior Administrative Assistant needed. The successful candidate will be professional, flexible and comfortable walking into a new situation and getting to work immediately. Dependability, ability to multi-task and attention to detail is important to your success in this job. Additional requirements follow.

Responsibilities
• Screen and direct incoming phone calls to appropriate recipients.
• Greet and direct visitors.
• Maintain company database.
• Perform simple project coordination, including copying, collating, binding, packaging and distributing various reports and other documents.
• Filing
• Data entry (6000 KPH + preferred).
• Report tracking.

Requirements:
• Bachelor's degree preferred.
• 2 years administrative/clerical experience.
• Excellent working knowledge of MS Office (Word, Excel, PowerPoint, Outlook).
• Typing speed 50 WPM.
• Excellent verbal and written communication skills.
• Able to work independently with little direction.

Even with a small sample, a clear picture of what this job really entails becomes apparent. Have a look at the completed Key Element Detector™ (Figure 3).

Notice how often the soft skills are mentioned: "communication skills", "detail oriented", "organized" and even "professionalism", "dependability" and "flexibility". It would be safe to deduce that for administrative jobs, the ability to get along with others and being responsible are key elements. Pay attention to the

Proof on Resumes

Proof on your resume answers the "what can you do" and "where have you done it" questions. It is the concrete elements on your resume – exact dates, locations, company names, college names, etc. This critical information is universal to every resume.

For example, each job in your work history should list the position title, company name, location and dates in the first line. This is the proof of your claims, the concrete evidence. If a statement has no proof, the HR people don't count it. Not only that, but if HR can't see it in the first 30 seconds, it doesn't count either.

Consider this sample: what caused the candidate to be screened out?

Figure 4.1: Proof on resumes

> **NEW APPLICANT**
> Some city, USA, fakeemail@yahoo.com, 303-555-1212
>
>
> **SUMMARY:**
> Enthusiastic public relations professional with a desire to create effective publicity campaigns for non-profit corporations.
>
> **EDUCATION:**
> University of State, City, USA
> Bachelors of Arts, May 2007
>
>
> **EXPERIENCE:**
> **Public Relations Intern, Big Hospital, City, USA**
> Wrote articles for the internal publication and quarterly magazine. Compile the weekly email bag for distribution to all employees. Plan, organize, and carry out special events. Escort media throughout the hospital for photo shoots and press conferences. 6/07 -01/08
>
> **Office Assistant, The PR Company, City, USA**
> Worked directly with non-profit members by assisting fundraising needs. Compose stories with photos and details regarding specific member events that are available to the public. Build strong relationships with clients and organizations. Update files and contact lists. 9/05 – 10/07
>
> **Special Events Assistant, Non-Profit Company, City, USA**
> Assisted the Director of Special Events in organizing the company's largest fundraising event of the year. Worked with donors, board members and vendors. 01/04– 06/04

Did you see the dates of employment? Neither would the HR department. This resume will go directly to the rejection pile because the proof was not easily accessible in a 30-second reading.

A Great Truth

Good resumes show the vital information quickly. A hiring manager should always see the dates, titles, employer's names and locations within 30 seconds.

Creating emphasis on resumes

What are your best assets? How do you get them across? Emphasis has nothing to do with fonts, bolding, italics and so on. When you lose your formatting, you only have the words left to make your point. To combat this problem, emphasis is shown by how the sections are arranged (placement) and by how much you write (volume).

Placement
Items and sections listed first on the resume have the most emphasis.

Volume
The more you write about something, the more emphasis it carries.

No matter which resume style you choose, you can always change the order of information. This gives you freedom to move things around for different effects. For example, a new college graduate who wants to emphasize his degree would list it first on the resume. An executive would list her profile and work experience first. Education goes last on the executive's resume, since her work history, accomplishments and skills are all more relevant than an older degree.

Use intelligent placement on your resume. Be sure to utilize what you learned from the Key Element Detector™. The results can tell you what you should emphasize. For example, some jobs are skill-based, such as an executive assistant; since skills matter most, the skill set comes first. Other jobs are results-driven, such as project management; this requires concrete results emphasized throughout the work history.

One emphasis trick – Use capitals

On the Word document, you will still use bold or italics as the visual element on your resume. However, if you use capital letters at the same time, it will carry through on a text conversion. Using ALL CAPITALS for your headings is a great way to keep your resume flowing and to show breaks for different sections.

You may have heard that writing in all capitals is equivalent to screaming at the reader, and that is true – in cover letters and emails. Don't be afraid to use them in your resume as a way to overcome the difficulties with text conversions.

Figure 4.2: Capitalized work history in Word documents

If you use ALL CAPITALS at section headers or titles, it helps with text conversions...

SALES EXECUTIVE, XYZ Company, Denver, CO 2003 – present
Created long-term B2B sales relationships with new clientele
- Increased sales by 10% for three consecutive years

CUSTOMER ADVOCATE, BC Company, Denver, CO 2000 – 2003
Worked closely with clients to ensure highest level of personalized customer service
- Increased sales by suggesting upgrades on materials and services

Text conversion with capitals
Notice how the capitals help guide the reader through important section or information changes:

```
SALES EXECUTIVE, XYZ Company, Denver, CO  2003 - present
Created long-term B2B sales relationships with new
clientele
Increased sales by 10% for three consecutive years

CUSTOMER ADVOCATE, BC Company, Denver, CO  2000 - 2003
Worked closely with clients to ensure highest level of
personalized customer service
Increased sales by suggesting upgrades on materials and
services
```

While the text version is certainly not as pretty as the Word version, using capitals for the job title gives the reader a visual separation. Adding this simple touch makes your material easier to understand in the critical 30-second reading.

* * *

Typical resume sections and how to use them

Since emphasis is show by moving the different sections around, it is important to know the purpose and intent behind each particular section.

Figure 4.3 shows the basic anatomy of a resume - please note that some of the detail has been omitted or simplified to fit within the page of this book. In reality, the resume would typically be two pages long and include more detail to pass an HR screening.

Contact information

Resumes always start with your contact information, including your name, address, phone numbers and even your LinkedIn.com profile. I know what you're thinking: "duh!" But I have seen resumes where the candidate forgot to put his phone number on his resume.

Always keep your contact information easy to find. Your email address should be kept professional; no ladiesman626@email.com, please. If you need to, create an address based on your name through a free service such as Yahoo, Hotmail or Gmail. Adding your LinkedIn URL is a growing trend, although still not necessary. However, if you are in an industry that adopts new technology easily, you may want to include it.

One of the more recent evolutions of resumes is to exclude your physical home address. Some of this is to combat scam job listings. If you are worried about listing the home address on the resume because of identity theft concerns, you can list just your phone numbers and email address. Just keep in mind that when you fill out an online application, you will have to provide your mailing address.

Another possible reason to omit the address is to increase your chances if you are relocating to a different city. Employers tend to favor local candidates; omitting an address may help in getting past this stumbling block.

Figure 4.3: Anatomy of a Resume

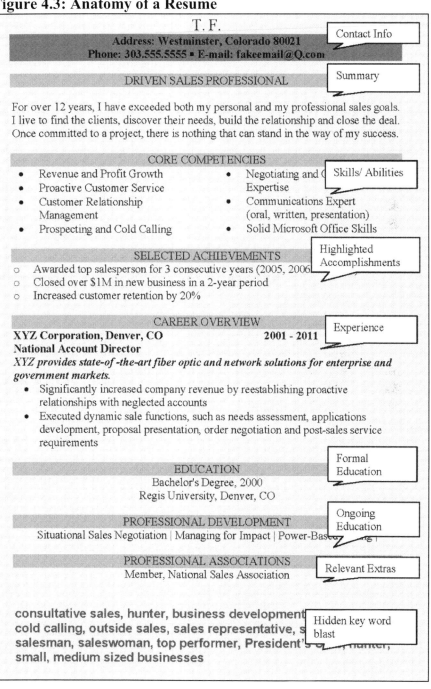

T. F.

Address: Westminster, Colorado 80021
Phone: 303.555.5555 ▪ E-mail: fakeemail@Q.com

Contact Info

DRIVEN SALES PROFESSIONAL

Summary

For over 12 years, I have exceeded both my personal and my professional sales goals. I live to find the clients, discover their needs, build the relationship and close the deal. Once committed to a project, there is nothing that can stand in the way of my success.

CORE COMPETENCIES

- Revenue and Profit Growth
- Proactive Customer Service
- Customer Relationship Management
- Prospecting and Cold Calling

- Negotiating and *Skills/ Abilities* Expertise
- Communications Expert (oral, written, presentation)
- Solid Microsoft Office Skills

SELECTED ACHIEVEMENTS

Highlighted Accomplishments

- Awarded top salesperson for 3 consecutive years (2005, 2006
- Closed over $1M in new business in a 2-year period
- Increased customer retention by 20%

CAREER OVERVIEW

Experience

XYZ Corporation, Denver, CO   2001 - 2011
National Account Director
XYZ provides state-of-the-art fiber optic and network solutions for enterprise and government markets.

- Significantly increased company revenue by reestablishing proactive relationships with neglected accounts
- Executed dynamic sale functions, such as needs assessment, applications development, proposal presentation, order negotiation and post-sales service requirements

EDUCATION

Formal Education

Bachelor's Degree, 2000
Regis University, Denver, CO

PROFESSIONAL DEVELOPMENT

Ongoing Education

Situational Sales Negotiation | Managing for Impact | Power-Base

PROFESSIONAL ASSOCIATIONS

Relevant Extras

Member, National Sales Association

consultative sales, hunter, business development
cold calling, outside sales, sales representative, s
salesman, saleswoman, top performer, President'
small, medium sized businesses

Hidden key word blast

41

Profiles / Summaries / Passion Statements

Profiles or summaries replace the old-fashioned Objective statements. When you list the title of the job you want at the beginning of the section, this lets HR know your employment goal without resorting to the hated Objective statement. (And yes, HR really does hate those objectives.)

Summaries show up to three of your top attributes for any job. Why are you the best candidate? What do you have to offer? Another variety of this is the Passion Statement, which talks about your why you love your job - phrased in relevant key words. We'll show you how to create a Passion Statement in Chapter 5.

Summaries should not be longer than three sentences. Don't waste time vamping away; they won't read a long, drawn-out personal history. Be short, be clear and be powerful.

Skill Set (a.k.a. Skill Summary, Technical Skills, Personal Assets and Core Competencies)

Skill sets list your technical abilities and personal assets that relate to the job. These should come directly from your Key Element Detector™, although you can certainly dress up the language to keep it interesting. Just don't get *too* creative... Hiring managers and HR departments will read this section and tick off how many of your skills match their needs. If the key words don't match, you could easily get screened out.

The beauty of a solid skill set is its brief nature. This section should never include long, drawn out sentences with big explanations. Be short and to-the-point. You want them to see your value quickly.

One variation is the Core Competencies: these are carefully chosen job titles, functions or attributes. Many mid- to upper-management resumes use this technique. In addition to drawing attention, they create more key words to pass screening or to stand out in resume searches.

If your Key Element Detector™ shows an emphasis on titles over skills, using Core Competencies are a great way to draw them into your resume. Some positions in particular draw this type of job definition – sales, for example. In that case, the Core Competencies tend to use intangible skills, such as "goal-oriented" and "proven results."

Key Achievements (a.k.a. Career Highlights)

The key achievements section is a synopsis of your successes or results. Written in sentence form, these lines can cover the accomplishment with some detail. Like Core Competencies, they are frequently used on mid- to upper-level positions. They can be very effective for result-oriented jobs, such as sales or marketing. Achievements can help define a diverse career history.

Warning: Several hiring managers and HR people have a big gripe about the key achievements section. All too often, people separate their accomplishments from their work history. Hiring managers have to guess about what deed goes with which job. And remember, every time you let someone assume things on your resume, it will go against you.

A better tactic is to list your accomplishments under the heading of a particular position:

Correct way to list achievements – under a job heading

National Sales Manager
XYZ Company, Faketown, USA 2004-2008
Responsible for leading a team of 25 Salespersons in a 3-Region territory. Continued to service major national accounts.
- Named Top Salesman in the Northwest Region 2004 & 2007
- Increased customer base by 10% for 3 consecutive years
- Consistently met and exceeded Team Sales goals

See how much this adds to the job? Landing the accomplishment in your work history section enhances the work history and increases the reader's appreciation.

The Great Key Accomplishments Debate

Plenty of recruiters, resume writers and managers will defend the stand-alone list of accomplishments. It was a clever marketing technique concocted in the 1990s and many still like to use it. Recent research states that younger managers don't have a problem with the disconnected accomplishments, while older managers prefer the accomplishments tied to a job.

> Consider this: if you know a significant portion of your target audience is going to dislike your presentation, why would you risk it?

Work History (a.k.a. Professional Experience, Work Experience)
Employers are very interested in what you've done and where you did it. It is critical that they get this information in a clear, concise and effective manner. Don't play games here – you need to follow specific formatting rules in this section.

First of all, the dates, company name, location and job title must be listed at the beginning of every job. You can play with the order, such as leading with the job title, company name or the dates of employment. The order doesn't matter, but *all* of the information must be there. That is what HR departments and hiring managers are looking for!

Think of your work history as a skeletal system. Everything is built on the bones. Your bones are the critical information points. Then muscles are attached to them – for resumes, your muscles are the duties, achievements and/or results for each job. Even adding a sentence about what the company did can add strength to the presentation.

If your background includes different career paths, experience can be split into relevant experience and other /additional experience sections (see Figure 4.4). This is an effective tool if you are re-entering a field after a gap, or if you are making a career transition.

In this example, the candidate is emphasizing his sales experience. The radio work is interesting, and he doesn't want a gap in employment, but his real focus is sales. Presented this way, the resume tells the hiring manager that the candidate is serious about sales.

With either format, each section should have the work history listed chronologically, with the most current listed first. It is generally accepted to limit your work history to 10-20 years.

Figure 4.4: How to list additional experience

WORK EXPERIENCE:
National Sales Manager, XYZ Company, USA 2004-2008
Responsible for leading a team of 25 salespersons in a three-region territory. Continued to service major national accounts.
- Top salesman in the Northwest region 2004 & 2007
- Increased customer base by 10% for three consecutive years

Regional Sales Representative, ABC Company, Faketown, USA 2002 – 2004
Successfully sold a new line of widgets in the Northwestern region.
- Awarded the Golden Widget for outstanding sales results, 2003

Sales Associate, GHL Company, Faketown, USA   1995 – 1998
Conducted business-to-business sales of sophisticated accounting programs for companies with gross annual revues above $10M
- Consistently exceeded sales goals by 5-7% per year

ADDITIONAL EXPERIENCE:
On-air Personality, MNO Radio, Faketown, USA 1998 – 2002
Hosted overnight radio program. Responsible for running all advertising. Maintained detailed logs for commercials, music and promotions.

Volunteer Experience

Whether you are in a distressed industry or not, volunteer experience can help fill employment gaps on your resume. Of course, volunteer work is more important than just giving you something to do while you're unemployed. Many people volunteer throughout their career. Regardless of your motives or time commitment levels, volunteer work does have its place on your resume.

Many employers like to see volunteer experience as a way to give back to the community, especially if your experience goes beyond a period of unemployment. Choose your volunteer activities carefully; helping update a volunteer data base has more career value than cleaning dog cages at the local animal shelter (unless, of course, you work in the pet care industry). However, don't fill up this resume section with overly trivial information. One past client of mine listed that she had participated in the local annual walk to raise funds for breast cancer research. Note - she only showed up on the day of the walk, bought a t-shirt, and walked in the 5-mile "fun run". While it was an important cause, this level of participation was hardly resume-worthy. If she had helped with the event set-up or gathered $10,000 worth of pledges, well, that's another story. But just doing a walk? To hiring managers, including such a limited level of involvement only casts doubt onto the rest of the resume; after all, if the candidate includes such minimal items, would she also exaggerate other areas of her resume?

The moral of the story: don't load up on trivial information that could distract from your professional message.

Education

Education can be a formal college degree or on-going training, classes or professional development. Like your work history, the school's name, location and degree information are critical pieces to include. High school is rarely listed, except for new college graduates or younger candidates who don't have a college degree. (If you are over 30, never list high school, regardless of whether you attended college or not.) Including information about your major, school activities or a sorority/fraternity can add value, but only if it is recent and relates to your field.

The Great Date Debate

Some older job seekers are reluctant to list their graduation date, fearing ageism will become a factor. Nobody wants to date themselves, especially if only 15 years of work history is shown but the degree was attained 30 years ago.

Some HR people won't acknowledge the degree without the date. On the other hand, some recruiters never list the graduation date.

Decide for yourself which is the greater risk – no date or no degree.

Remember, even if you choose not to list the date on your resume, online applications will force you to enter the date. Don't be surprised or totally disheartened if your choice is taken away. Most corporate recruiters are more understanding about this issue than you might think. (Still not convinced? See Chapter 7: Dealing with Discrepancies.)

Professional Associations

Professional associations and affiliations can add to your presentation. It shows connection and commitment to your industry. However, don't list anything that reveals your religious beliefs, political views, ethnicity or any other factor that could be protected under federal anti-discrimination laws. An exception to the rule is jobs within those areas; for example, a therapist wanting to work with the Salvation Army (a Christian-based non-profit organization) might list their Christian Therapist Association membership from college.

Keep this section brief. List their name and your dates of membership. To avoid confusion or misinterpretation of acronyms, write the name out.

While this section is helpful, your work history is more important. If you need to cut something down because space is short, shorten professional associations.

Professional Development

Professional Development consists of any ongoing education you have received *outside* of formal education. This can include workshops, coaching, individual instruction, areas of study and even professional conferences. The point is to show that you are committed to your professional growth.

Hidden Key Word Blast

First of all, in Figure 4.3: Anatomy of a Resume, you can see the hidden key word blast at the bottom of the resume. In reality, these terms are imbedded in the footer section of the resume *in white lettering on a white background.* This concept was specifically developed to get past computerized screening. By including every conceivable variation of the key words, the hope is that the resume will pop up in a search based on those terms. (Can you tell IT people came up with that one?)

This is not an absolute necessary, but if your Key Element Detector™ shows a lot of variance in the words chosen, the hidden key words may help your cause. If nothing else, you can use this same key word blast in your "Specialties" section of your LinkedIn.com summary.

References

If your industry is driven by references, go ahead and list three (or more) references by name, title and company on your resume. Including one or more personal references is a nice touch as well, especially if you want to show stability. If you are worried about disclosing too much, you can add the line, "contact information available on request."

Some online applications make you fill in all of the contact information right away. Don't be nervous about this. Nobody is going to call your references before they call you. No HR department has that much spare time. References are called when the job offer is imminent, and that won't happen before the interviews.

Are you lacking solid references or are you keeping your job search secret from your current employer? Past co-workers can serve as a reference, or friends who know you in a professional or volunteer capacity. Always think of ways to cultivate your references. They are an important part of your network.

* * *

Planning your resume sections

Now that you know how to use each of the sections, let's start building the framework for your resume. Below are listed the major sections for resumes. Next to each one, write the level of importance, starting with 1. Not all of the sections may be relevant; if is not appropriate for your situation, write "NA" for "non-applicable."

Tip: Summaries are either the first thing on the resume or the very last.

_____ Summary

_____ Skills - make the distinction between:
   Hard skills, such as computer programs
   Soft skills or personality traits, such as "team player"

_____ Key Achievements

_____ Work History

_____ Volunteer Experience

_____ Education

_____ Professional Development

_____ Professional Associations

_____ Extra tidbits or Interests (rare)

_____ Hidden key word blast

Now that you have your weighted list, build your resume by leading with your relevant strengths.

* * *

Common Resume Formats and Styles

I am a pretty simple person. In my mind, there really are only four types of resumes: a laundry list, a paragraph, an outline and the functional resume. Sure, you can change the appearance with different formatting tricks, but if you can understand how each resume style works, you can't really go wrong.

Some resumes may have aspects of all four, but this is simply an adaptation. Don't get overwhelmed by the various techniques other resume writers may use, like "experience-driven formal presentation" or "executive key achievement" resume. If you think about it, you have already determined the emphasis of your resume by understanding the order of your sections. That's all that professional resume writers are trying to say- oh, and use big terms to impress you.

The fact is that when resumes converted to text, they fall into one of the four basic resume styles. If you work within the formats from the beginning, less will be lost in text translation.

Don't let text fear rule your life

Many job seekers think they need to do the text version of their resume in addition to their Word document, in an attempt to control how the document will convert to text. This could be dangerous; once again, it creates multiple versions of the resume. It can be difficult to manage the numerous documents, especially if they are similar. Details can slide incredibly quickly.

Save yourself the headache. Let the employers' computers do the conversion. If you follow the guidelines here, your resume will convert to text just fine without any special adaptations. HR departments are used to the text-converted resumes. They deal with them all the time.

You can do a couple of simple tricks to help control the visual appearance of your resume. You can send out a PDF version, however, keep in mind that a PDF will not work for online applications. Another option is to save your document as a Rich Text Format (.rtf). The Rich Text Format will keep your font, indentions, bullets and other formatting in place, but computers still see it as text. It will look nice. But always keep in mind that online applications will not hold the formatting, no matter what you do.

Keep things simple. Above everything else, you need to be comfortable with your own materials. Rather than concentrating on the message, you spend too much time on the packaging. Resumes are a tool, not something to enslave you.

* * *

The Laundry List

A laundry list resume is a simple as its name suggests. It takes the duties, skills and other details and lists them in a logical format, frequently as bulleted points:

Figure 4.5: The Laundry List Resume

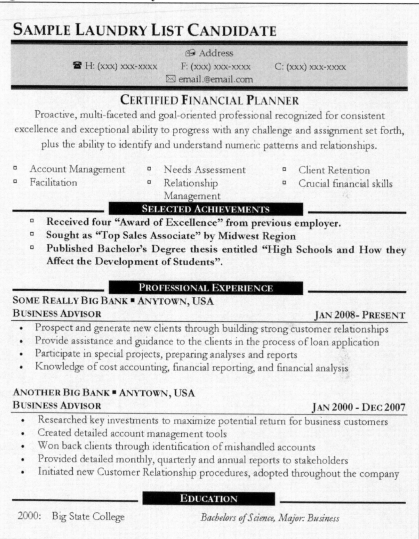

SAMPLE LAUNDRY LIST CANDIDATE

Address
☎ H: (xxx) xxx-xxxx   F: (xxx) xxx-xxxx   C: (xxx) xxx-xxxx
✉ email.@email.com

CERTIFIED FINANCIAL PLANNER

Proactive, multi-faceted and goal-oriented professional recognized for consistent excellence and exceptional ability to progress with any challenge and assignment set forth, plus the ability to identify and understand numeric patterns and relationships.

- Account Management
- Facilitation
- Needs Assessment
- Relationship Management
- Client Retention
- Crucial financial skills

SELECTED ACHIEVEMENTS

- **Received four "Award of Excellence" from previous employer.**
- **Sought as "Top Sales Associate" by Midwest Region**
- **Published Bachelor's Degree thesis entitled "High Schools and How they Affect the Development of Students".**

PROFESSIONAL EXPERIENCE

SOME REALLY BIG BANK ▪ ANYTOWN, USA
BUSINESS ADVISOR   JAN 2008- PRESENT

- Prospect and generate new clients through building strong customer relationships
- Provide assistance and guidance to the clients in the process of loan application
- Participate in special projects, preparing analyses and reports
- Knowledge of cost accounting, financial reporting, and financial analysis

ANOTHER BIG BANK ▪ ANYTOWN, USA
BUSINESS ADVISOR   JAN 2000 - DEC 2007

- Researched key investments to maximize potential return for business customers
- Created detailed account management tools
- Won back clients through identification of mishandled accounts
- Provided detailed monthly, quarterly and annual reports to stakeholders
- Initiated new Customer Relationship procedures, adopted throughout the company

EDUCATION

2000: Big State College   *Bachelors of Science, Major: Business*

Advantage:

Laundry List resumes read easily and get to the point without a lot of extra fluff. They also convert well to a text format.

Disadvantage:

These resumes are deceptively simple. Just think about it: the most difficult form of writing is poetry, because a limited number of words must convey the entire message. Laundry List resumes work the same way.

Figure 4.6: The Laundry List converted to text

SAMPLE LAUNDRY LIST CANDIDATE
Address
H: (xxx) xxx-xxxx   F: (xxx) xxx-xxxx   C: (xxx) xxx-xxxx
email.@email.com

CERTIFIED FINANCIAL PLANNER
Proactive, multi-faceted and goal-oriented professional
recognized for consistent excellence and exceptional ability to
progress with any challenge and assignment set forth.

Account Management
Facilitation
Needs Assessment
Relationship Management
Client Retention

SELECTED ACHIEVEMENTS
Received four "Award of Excellence" from previous employer.
Sought as "Top Sales Associate" by Midwest Region
Published Bachelor's Degree thesis entitled "High Schools and
How they Affect the Development of Students".

PROFESSIONAL EXPERIENCE
SOME REALLY BIG BANK - ANYTOWN, USA
BUSINESS ADVISOR
 JAN 2008- PRESENT
Prospect and generate new clients through building strong
customer relationships
Participate in special projects, preparing analyses and reports
Knowledge of cost accounting, financial reporting, and
financial analysis

ANOTHER BIG BANK - ANYTOWN, USA
BUSINESS ADVISOR
 JAN 2000 - DEC 2007
Researched key investments to maximize potential return for
business customers
Won back clients through identification of mishandled accounts
Provided detailed monthly, quarterly and annual reports to
stakeholders
Initiated new Customer Relationship procedures, adopted
throughout the company

EDUCATION
2000: Big State College Bachelors of Science, Major: Business

Traps:

Laundry Lists have three traps: not saying enough, saying too much or becoming parrots to the job description.

Figure 4.7: Laundry List traps

Trap #1 - too thin

Experience:

Administrative Assistant, NoName Company, '07-'09
- Answered phones
- Filed and sorted documents
- Helped with special projects

Trap #2 - too much

Experience:

Director, IT Systems Engineering, 2004 - 2009
SCF Company   Anytown, USA
- Delivered third-generation technology upgrade for Celera's high performance computing center on schedule and under budget. This upgrade improved capability at a $4.2 million lower cost per year. The project received a CIO 100 Award from *CIO Magazine* for business innovation.
- Partnered with the business management group to re-architect an international data services network to provide the same functionality at a reduced cost of $650 thousand per year.
- Collaborated in the development and rollout of governance processes, including portfolio management and project management life cycle, which improved alignment of IT systems with business goals, delivery and realization of benefits.
- Implemented a Systems Development Life Cycle to standardize the selection and delivery of new technology. These repeatable processes provided transparency to IT's efforts and allowed for better utilization of engineering resources, savings against project plans, and improved solutions.

Trap #3 – repeating the job description

Experience:

Tax Accountant, MSI Accounting, Faketown   2007-2009
- Prepared individual, corporate, partnership and not-for-profit income tax returns using Lacerte software.
- Prepared compiled financial statements for corporations and sole proprietors.
- Prepared quarterly and year-end payroll reports and quarterly gross receipts reports.

Trap #1: Too thin
In this sample, we can't get a feel for the job; there is just not enough information to make a judgment. In this case, HR departments will pass this candidate up in favor of someone whose experience they can identify.

Trap #2: Saying too much
While it is obvious that this job covered many key areas, the reader can't absorb the information. It's crowded and difficult to read. Worse, when converted to text, the bullets will be lost and all visual clues will be gone. All employers hate this, from the HR office to executive management.

Trap#3: Repeating the job description word-for-word
While very factual, resumes that repeat the job description are very boring. If the duties start with the same word for each bullet point, that's always a bad sign.

* * *

The Paragraph Resume
Paragraph Resumes are great for telling a detailed career history. Instead of lists, key points are written in paragraphs on the page, separated into sections. Paragraph Resumes are often favored by mid- to upper- management candidates because of the amount of detail they can fit in.

Advantage:
Hiring managers do tend to like this format. Many of them use this format themselves. These resumes highlight key achievements and results – both are important factors for management, marketing, information technology, sales and any career where the end result is king.

Disadvantage:
HR people don't like this format. It takes more time for them to wade through the information on the page, making it hard to judge within 60 seconds. Even worse, it loses a lot when converted to text, making it extremely difficult to follow:

Figure 4.8: The Paragraph Resume

Joe Schmoe
303-555-1212   bogusemail@yahoo.com

Career Summary

Results-oriented business professional with over 12 years of experience in business development, project management, business analysis, contract negotiation and vendor relationships. Expertise spans multiple industries including retail, financial services, healthcare and distribution. Key ability to communicate across business functions and all levels in an organization to achieve organizational goals.

Key Achievements

Business Development:
Senior Director of Sales and Strategy for a consulting services company with several service lines. Developed new business, including partner relationships, lead generation and follow-up, contract negotiations and client transfer of services to the delivery teams.

Program/ Project Management:
Performed manager responsibilities for multiple projects concurrently including project budget development and review, personnel issues, project plan management, and executive communications. Effectively delegated appropriate responsibility to project team

Work Experience

Technology Consultant, XYZ Company, Anytown USA   2000- Present
Key consultant for company specializing in forward-thinking technology solutions for a wide range of industries, including healthcare and governmental sources. Responsible for business development activities, business analysis, personnel management and project management of various levels.

Lead Manager, ABD Company, Anytown, USA   1995 - 1999
Responsible for a team of 15 in the Research & Development division. Organized required production schedules. Ensured crucial deadlines were met. Headed up company's professional development initiatives.

Education

MBA, Information Systems State University, Anytown, USA   2001
Focus of study included international market research and analysis, marketing channel development, partnership structures and corporate infrastructures

BS, Finance Other State University, Faketown, USA   1998

Figure 4.9: The Paragraph Resume text conversion

```
Joe Schmoe
303-555-1212
bogusemail@yahoo.com

Career Summary
Results-oriented business professional with over 12 years of
experience in business development, project management,
business analysis, contract negotiation and vendor
relationships.  Key ability to communicate across business
functions and all levels in an organization to achieve
organizational goals.

Key Achievements
Business Development:
Senior Director of Sales and Strategy for a consulting services
company with several service lines.  Developed new business,
including partner relationships, lead generation and follow-up,
contract negotiations and client transfer of services to the
delivery teams.

Program/ Project Management:
Performed manager responsibilities for multiple projects
concurrently including project budget development and review,
personnel issues, project plan management, and executive
communications.  Effectively delegated appropriate
responsibility to project team

Work Experience
Technology Consultant, XYZ Company, Anytown USA
2000- Present
Key consultant for company specializing in forward-thinking
technology solutions for a wide range of industries.
Responsible for business development activities, business
analysis, personnel management and project management of
various levels.

Lead Manager, ABD Company, Anytown, USA
1995 - 1999
Responsible for a team of 15 in the Research & Development
division.  Organized required production schedules. Headed up
company's professional development initiatives.

Education
MBA, Information Systems State University, Anytowm, USA 2001
BS, Finance State University, Faketown, USA, 1998
```

Traps:

Saying too much and unattached accomplishments.   Unlinked
accomplishments can slip into being a functional resumes, a problem
we will dive into soon enough.

Figure 4.10: Paragraph Resume trap - Saying too much

Private Academy for Troubled Youth   *Anytown, USA*
<u>*Teacher*</u> May 2003 to June 2005
Work with boys of varying abilities, including special education requirements, on a daily basis to modify behavior and/or increase educational achievement. Create lesson plans and curriculum, implement those plans, leave substitute and emergency plans, find resources, and grade papers for Aggression Replacement Training, College Psychology 101 and 102, and monitor one block of in-school detention daily. Previous classes have been Building Language Skills and High School Psychology. Act as educational advocate for a caseload of twelve to fourteen boys, participating in their treatment team meetings, daily guided feedback sessions, and write semester reports documenting their progress. Carry a special education caseload, including Individualized education plans for a unit on campus. Computer programs utilized: Access, Excel, Word, TRAILS, email, Internet

Saying too much is overwhelming to the reader. No one will wade through this amount of detail. Forget about them making an accurate judgment in 60 seconds. If your slug lines don't grab them, they won't bother to read the rest. Remember, the point of the resume is to entice the managers to call you, not to give your life story.

* * *

The Outline Resume
In an Outline format, positions start with a summary, followed by aspects emphasized with indentions, bullets or both. Bulleted points can be arranged into sub-sets, or on occasion, the results or accomplishment for the subset.

Advantage:
This format reads really well in the first 60 seconds. Outlines are especially well suited to developing logic trains, because the logical information placement flows naturally. An outline resume drops to text relatively easy, similar to a laundry list, because of the frequent introductions of new lines.

Figure 4.11: The Outline Resume

SAMPLE OUTLINE CANDIDATE
123 Fake St, Anytown, USA
Tel: 303-555-5555   fakeemail@fake.com

INTERNATIONAL SALES MANAGER

Highly effective sale professional with 10+ years experience in diverse international markets. Deep understanding of cultural diversity necessary to develop long- term business partnerships.

CORE COMPETENCIES:

Strategic Planning & Solutions	International Business Development
Product Management	Market Research
Leadership	Project Management
Excellent Communication Skills	International Presentations
Results-Oriented	Innovative

Proven experience in **Europe, Japan, Asia Pacific, Australia, the Middle East, Canada, Mexico, Latin America and the Caribbean.** Knowledgeable in both operations and strategic planning. Expertise in international customs, negotiations, legal and cultural considerations.

PROFESSIONAL EXPERIENCE:

Director, International Sales and Marketing   **July 2008 - Present**
Some Company - Anytown, USA
This company is the maker of a wonderful product that dominates the pet market. Markets include Veterinary, Institutional, Governmental, Health Care and Retail.
 Personally responsible for the Global Brand Expansion. Developed significant channels into 30 new countries. Taught effective marketing techniques, international procedures and other practices to various departments in the emerging company.
- Developed significant distribution channels, including a 3-year, $5M contract
- Expanded customer base in 30 new countries since July 2008
- Lead 3 successful domestic campaigns
- Added 40 new trade customers in 12 months, increasing sales by 390%
- Significant involvement with Marketing Group:
  - Helped marketing group develop an effective 2-year plan
  - Launched channel-specific and country-specific labeling and marketing programs for 17 countries

EDUCATION:

MBA, State University, 2008	BA, State College, 2004
Graduated with Distinction	Graduated with Honors
International Business and Marketing	Business Administration and Management

OUTREACH PROGRAMS AND COMMUNITY INVOLVEMENT:

- Canadian Trade Ambassador: NAFTA Trade Discussion panelist
- Taiwan Trade Ambassador: Exporting to Taiwan ITC forum panelist

Disadvantage:

Since Outlines are really crossbreeds of Paragraphs and Laundry List styles, it could have the same problems as both of them. Wordy summaries won't convert well to text. Bulleted highlights need to be high-impact statements.

58

Figure 4.12: The Outline Resume text conversion

```
SAMPLE OUTLINE CANDIDATE
123 Fake St, Anytown, USA
Tel: 303-555-5555
fakeemail@fake.com

INTERNATIONAL SALES MANAGER
Highly effective sale professional with 10+ years experience in
diverse international markets.
Deep understanding of cultural diversity necessary to develop
long- term business partnerships.

CORE COMPETENCIES:
 Strategic Planning & Solutions
 Product Management
 Leadership
 Excellent Communication Skills
 Results-Oriented


Proven experience in Europe, Japan, Asia Pacific, Australia,
the Middle East, Canada, Mexico, Latin America and the
Caribbean.  Knowledgeable in both operations and strategic
planning.  Expertise in international customs, negotiations,
legal and cultural considerations.

PROFESSIONAL EXPERIENCE:
Director, International Sales and Marketing, July 2008 -
Present
Some Company - Anytown, USA
Personally responsible for the Global Brand Expansion.
Developed significant channels into 30 new countries.  Taught
effective marketing techniques, international procedures and
other practices to various departments in the emerging company.
Developed significant distribution channels, including a 3-
year, $5M contract
Expanded customer base in 30 new countries since July 2008
Lead 3 successful domestic campaigns
Significant involvement with Marketing Group:
Helped marketing group develop an effective 2-year plan
Launched channel-specific and country-specific labeling and
marketing programs for 17 countries

EDUCATION:
BA, State College, 2004
Graduated with Honors
Business Administration and Management
```

Trap: Getting too clever

The biggest trap for Outline Resumes is creating overly complex formatting. In this case, the advantages gained start getting lost. The cascading information can easily be misinterpreted in the 30-second reading:

Figure 4.13: Outline Resume Trap - Getting too clever

Director, IT Systems Engineering, *Company Confidential*
Anytown, USA   2004-2006
Responsible for the design and implementation of information
technology solutions for a global biotechnology company, managing
projects of $12 – 15 million and a team of 28 people geographically
distributed across the U.S.

- Participated in the transformation of the information
  technology organization to meet the needs of a large and
  complex corporation.
  - Delivered systems capabilities to support strategy and
    drive business growth.
- Delivered third-generation technology upgrade for Celera's
  high performance computing center on schedule and under
  budget.
  - Upgrade improved capability at a $4.2 million lower
    cost per year.
    - Project received a CIO 100 Award from *CIO
      Magazine* for business innovation.
- Partnered with the business management group to re-
  architect an international data services network to provide
  the same functionality
  - Reduced cost of $650 thousand per year.

In general, if your nested information goes three levels deep, it
is probably too complex.

* * *

The Functional Resume
Technically, a functional resume can be any of the other three resume
types. The "functional" aspect is the attempt to highlight the
candidate's functions or skills within a job over their actual experience.

There are few situations when this type of resume is
appropriate, most notably:

- When you have done the same thing in every job

- Your relevant experience is not current - that is, you are trying to re-enter into a previous field or job
- Your experience is limited

If you choose to use a functional resume, be aware that it is one of the formats disliked by both HR and hiring managers. In fact, in December 2010, the USA Today released a survey of 150 hiring managers across the country; 75% of them *disliked* the functional resume format.

So what is with the revulsion towards this resume format?

A Great Truth

Everyone hates functional resumes because they are frequently used by someone trying to hide something: their age, spotty work history or some other issue. When HR people see a functional resume, they will not take the time to decipher the work history. They give it 30 seconds, assume the candidate is hiding something, and move on.

A purely functional resume only lists key accomplishments, which are completely disconnected from the work history. The HR person and the hiring manager must assume everything. They can't be certain about what duties you were doing on each job, because all of the duties and accomplishments are not listed with each particular job.

Using a functional resume appropriately

Keep in mind that a proper functional resume is really only appropriate when you did the exact job over and over again. Look at the sample Functional Resume in Figure 4.14. In this case, the job of a private chef for a yacht literally is the same job on every boat (uh, excuse me, ship). The chef is responsible for preparing the meals, getting supplies, keeping things clean and creating special events. In this case, we *can* list the duties as their own section, followed by the details of which ships she served on. If you look closely, you can also note that this is technically a Laundry List resume with a Paragraph opening:

61

Figure 4.14: The Functional Resume

Joe Schmoe
Someemail.com
303-555-5555
Ft. Lauderdale, Fl

Experienced Private Chef
Highly skilled Chef, with a drive to make your dining experience a creative delight at every meal. My career has been defined by dedicated service to others, as well as high quality foods personalized to the flavor profiles of my principals. Being a successful private chef means more than just creating perfect meals; it means being in tune with my employers' desires and anticipating their needs. This is the art of private service.

Personal Assets:
- 10+ Years of Private & Personal Chef Experience
- Decorated Army combat veteran
- Extremely hard working, accommodating and flexible
- Dedicated to life-long learning and professional development
- Upholds the highest confidentiality levels
- Consistently passes extensive background and security checks

Private Yacht Experience:
Executive Private Chef Responsibilities:
- Extensive provisioning in remote and international locations
- Menu development and planning
- Maintains meticulous sanitation and cleanliness standards
- Upholds Health and Safety procedures required for any sea voyage
- Caters events both on and off-board, including showcases and corporate events
- Prepared all meals for up to 14 crew members
- Ensure the galley, cabinet and storage areas are fully stocked
- Coordinate equipment deliveries and installations at international ports
- Direct management of sous chef; works closely with other crew members

Yacht Assignments:

2008 - Present	M/Y The Big Boat	150ft	11 Guests/ 12 Crew
2005 - 2006	M/Y No Its a Ship	150ft	12 Guests/ 9 Crew
2004 - 2005	M/Y Use the Right Term	150ft	12 Guests/ 7 Crew
2000 - 2003	M/Y LandLubber	106ft	10 Guests / 5 Crew

Education:

1999:	Culinary Institute of America	Hyde Park, NY	Associates in Occupational Studies

A big disadvantage:
A Functional Resume cannot auto-populate the fields on an automated applicant tracking system. In that case, very few humans will get to

see this resume at all. The computer cuts them before a person has a chance.

If you choose to use a Functional Resume, you will need to manually add the specific duties with each job. If you don't, the resume will get automatically filtered into the rejection pile.

* * *

Using computer resume templates
Many word processing programs contain resume templates, and you can get free ones online. If you want to use a template, go ahead – but look out for an important trap. As you fill out the different section of the template, your writing can start to sound robotic. This is especially true if you use one of the big employment websites to create your resume. Computers will only guide you through the process. They won't tell you when you're writing poorly.

Another issue is the text conversions. Several templates use text boxes to arrange the sections. While it looks great on paper, it can confuse the receiving computer. Computers don't read the rows across like a human. They read them *down first, then over (see Figure 4.15, next page).*

So why are there so many resume templates that cause problems when they convert to text? Because these templates were designed by *graphic artists, NOT HR professionals.* As a result, they do not know how receiving computers will interpret the information. If you are working with a professional resume writer, make sure that he or she understands how HR will use the information.

Sample follows...

Figure 4.15: Problems with computer templates

Text Box Lines are made visible for this example - a normal template would only show dashed lines to indicate where the different table cells are:

Skills:	Proficient in Microsoft Office
	Excellent communication skills
	Team-oriented and dependable
Education:	Bachelor of Arts, 2008
	Some City College, USA
Experience:	Administrative Assistant, 2008 - Present
	XYQ Company, Some City, USA
	• Assisted with a variety of research projects, including document organization and drafting
	• Answered eight incoming phone lines
	• Responsible for office supplies

Template text conversion

When converted, receiving computers read information down, then over. This creates confusion in the text conversion...

Skills:
Education:
Experience:
Proficient in Microsoft Office
Excellent communication skills
Team-oriented and dependable
Bachelor of Arts, 2008
Some City College, USA
Administrative Assistant, 2008 - Present
XYQ Company, Some City, USA
Assisted with a variety of research projects, including document organization and drafting
Answered eight incoming phone lines
Responsible for office supplies

Formatting with tabs

Similarly, if you are using the tab key to align the sections on your resume, receiving computers will not recognize these. Use the indents instead. Indents are at set increments on the Word document.

With tabs, your Word document would look like Figure 4.16.:

All those crazy extra spaces are the tabs or extra spaces used to line things up in the Word document. These drive both HR people and hiring managers absolutely nuts. Use proper formatting techniques, which are indentations.

Figure 4.16 Format using tabs

Some people use the "tab" key or a series of individual "space bar" to line up resume information...

SKILLS:	Proficient in Microsoft Office
	Excellent communication skills
	Team-oriented and dependable
EDUCATION:	Bachelor of Arts, 2008
	Some City College, USA
EXPERIENCE:	Administrative Assistant, 2008 - Present
	XYQ Company, Some City, USA
	Assisted with a variety of research projects, including
	document organization and drafting
	Answered 8 incoming phone lines

However, in text, it converts to this:

SKILLS: Proficient in Microsoft Office   Excellent communication skills   Team-oriented and dependable

EDUCATION: Bachelor of Arts, 2008   Some City College, USA

EXPERIENCE: Administrative Assistant, 2008 - Present   XYQ Company, Some City, USA   Assisted with a variety of research projects, including   document organization and drafting   Answered 8 incoming phone lines

If anybody wants to work with this resume, they have to delete each tab and space individually - which takes a long, long time.

* * *

Creative options

Some industries are open to creative resume formats. In fact, some demand it. If you are in a creative industry, then the visual appearance of the resume becomes even more important. It is a sample of your work.

Figure 4.17 shows a resume created with imbedded tables and lines Do be careful, though. If you create something like this resume, be sure you know how to use it, including how to update it and how to apply to jobs with it. That's why I'm not telling you how to do it - if you are not good enough in Word to make something like this, it will drive you crazy!

Figure 4.17: A Creative Resume

J. Schmoe

123 Fake St ● Springfield, USA ● Phone: 720-555-5555 ● fakeemail@yahoo.com

Skills:

Microsoft Word,
Excel PowerPoint

Data base
programs such as
Business
Search/ ERIC;

Statistical Software
Mintab and
Qualtrics;

Project
coordination

Vendor
management

Data entry

Report creation

Personal Assets:

Detail-oriented

Analytical

Creative

Organized

Flexible

Determined

Marketing Professional

For me, I possess the unique ability to be able to analyze and understand a vast amount of marketing data while never losing sight of the big picture.

Education:

Bachelor of Science in Marketing, Dec. 2010
State College, Anytown, CO
- President of Colligate Entrepreneur's Organization
- 2009 recipient, Academic Award for Excellence

Certification, "Protecting Human Research Participants
National Institute of Health (NIH), Office of Extramural Research

Internships & Special Projects:

SBDC Strategic Analysis Project, 2010
Benefiting the Spiffy Car Wash, Anytown, CO
Created a 70-page report and presentation addressing an in-depth industry analysis, market conditions, general environmental analysis, Five Force analysis, industry competitiveness and recommendations.

Exploratory Research Report, 2010
Creative Media, Anytown, CO
Designed survey, collected data, analyzed and interpreted results and offered final recommendations.

Work Experience:

Adminstrative Assistant, 2006 - Present
ABC Company, Anytown, CO
Provides support to a busy, 10-person division. Manages 5 incoming phone lines, file organization, supplies and greets guests.

Final words on formats

No matter what resume format you use, it should make sense to you. It should flow logically and naturally, without too much stretching of the imagination. Make your message clear, concise and to-the-point, and choose the right format to uphold that image.

Chapter 5 - Let's Write that Resume!

At this point, I am sure that you are chomping at the bit to get to work on your resume. Okay, so maybe you are not exactly jumping for joy. But thanks to your completed Key Element Detector™, you know the right focus. Planning your resume sections gave you a roadmap. Based on your emphasis, you should have an idea of what format you want to use. The rest should be a snap, right?

Except for one thing: most people find it very difficult to write about themselves. If this is part of your challenge, don't feel bad. Most of my resume clients are in the same boat. I have even helped recruiters with their resumes - and they see hundreds of resumes every day. But when it comes to creating their own, they freeze up.

Part of the problem is the "bragging factor." It's hard to talk about your job in grandiose terms. People get so caught up in what they do every day that it creates a blind spot, the "it's no big deal" mentality. But here's the thing: what is commonplace to you is mysterious to others, especially recruiters who may not be familiar with your particular discipline. In that case, your resume is just as much a teaching tool as it is a statement of how great you are. It doesn't have to be a showboating document.

So what do employers really need to know?

Answer the three big questions

First and foremost, your resume is not about you; it's about the employer and his needs. Never forget that focus. To that end, every single employer cares about the same three things.

You must address these unspoken questions:

1. <u>What can you do?</u>
   You need to show your talents, but only the ones that employers care about. Stay focused on their needs, as revealed with the Key Element Detector. The rest is fluff, or worse, gives an impression that you want to pursue other interests.

2. <u>Where have you done it?</u>

This can be from your past work experience or through your education, or both. If you leave them guessing, you are going to lose.

3. <u>How does it apply to their needs?</u>
Every job posting in the universe reflects a specific function that employers need to fill. If you aren't answering that need, they aren't going to waste time on you.

If you cannot answer these three questions within 30 seconds, you will not get very far in the hiring process. Plus, most candidates fail to address the third issue. If you can keep your resume relevant to their needs, you gain a significant competitive advantage over the other job seekers.

Honesty is the best policy
Through your Key Element Detector, you know what your targeted employers are looking for. It might be tempting to pad your resume with those key words, even if you don't possess that skill or degree.

Don't do it!

Number one, false statements on your resume can be grounds for immediate dismissal. Number two, if you lie about your abilities, how can you perform the job?

Be true to yourself. Don't tell people what they want to hear. If you do, you will not discover the job that's best for you.

My philosophy is to find the right job, not just the "right now" job. This requires honesty at every phase – on the resume, in the interview and especially with yourself. You don't need to hide from less-than-ideal situations in your work history. Part of writing a resume is to reconcile with your past to prepare for the future. (See Chapter 7 Dealing with Discrepancies for suggestions on specific scenarios.) If you take the time to see things from a potential employer's point-of-view, you can begin to let go of the pain. This creates a new confidence, based on being able to discuss even a messy past without trying to hide. Remember, confident people are very attractive to future employers.

The Passion Statement: Keystone of your resume

Smart managers want to hire someone who is passionate about what they do. There are a number of reasons for this. Passionate employees are more engaged, tend to work harder, have less absenteeism and stay in the job longer. When all things are equal between candidates - skills, experience and education - the hiring manager will take the person who is excited to do the job. They have even been known to choose the passionate candidate *over* the more qualified ones.

So why not tell the hiring managers your passion in your resume and cover letter?

It's a bold move, which makes some people uncomfortable. It's easy to write the standard "results-oriented professional with 10 years of experience in creating highly effective teams." It's safe. It's comfortable.

And it also won't impress anybody.

In this crowded job market, you need to go beyond safe and comfortable to make a good impression. A resume that sounds just like everybody else is not unique.

This is why the Passion Statement is so important. A Passion Statement is a three-sentence summary of what you love about your job, expressed in key words and phrases that HR and managers will recognize. That's the real trick: it's not enough to say your zeal; it also has to be in key words.

Sample passion statement for a salesperson:

For over 12 years, I have exceeded both my personal and my professional sales goals. I live to find the clients, discover their needs, build the relationship and close the deal. Once committed to a project, there is nothing that can stand in the way of my success.

Doesn't that sound more intriguing than the "results-oriented professional"?

Hey! There's an "I" in there!

That's right - the Passion Statement is the ONLY place in your resume that you can use the "I" word. If it gets repeated or used in other sections, it is considered unprofessional and very amateurish. Why?

70

It's redundant. Everyone knows that everything on your resume refers to you, so the "I did..." is implied in every other sentence or bullet point. However, the Passion Statement requires the "I" word - its part of the uniqueness that helps you stand out.

Finding your passion

The first step for any Passion Statement is to figure out what you really do love about your job. Take a moment and consider your favorite job. Why did you like this job? What made you excited to go to work every day? These can be specific duties, projects or responsibilities. Maybe it was being a leader, or the people you worked with. Maybe it was getting to use unique skills or learning new things. Brainstorm as many different things about the job that you can:

_____

_____

_____

_____

I know what some of you are thinking already: what if I'm not passionate about the job? What if I'm just applying for this stuff so I don't starve while I look for a new career? That's fine - not every job we take is the love of our life. But you do need to find *something* that you enjoyed about a job and focus on that. For example, one of my clients had a "Plan B" job in retail management. Certainly not her love, but it paid the bills. After some serious thought and open brainstorming, we determined that she liked meeting new people and being helpful. And taking breaks. While we won't use "taking breaks" in her resume, we can build on the customer service aspects.

The Passion Statement formula

While highly personalized, Passion Statements do follow a very specific formula. Each sentence has its own focus (see Figure 5.1: Passion Statement Formula). Here's the magic bullet that makes this work: all of these passions use important key phrases that you discovered with your Key Element Detector™.

Figure 5.1

First sentence - years of experience and one core screening criteria:
_____

_____

Second sentence - what you really love about your job:
_____

_____

Third sentence - a personality trait that makes you ideal for this job:
_____

_____

Let's take a closer look at our sample Passion Statement for the experienced salesperson.

The first sentence, "for over 12 years, I have exceeded both my personal and my professional sales goals." We always start with the years of experience because that is one of HR's major screening criteria. Next is the core screening criteria; in sales, reaching and exceeding goals is what all hiring managers want.

Sentence two: "I live to find the clients, discover their needs, build the relationship and close the deal." Each one of these steps came straight from the Key Element Detector™. But even more important than that, these are the aspects of the job that this candidate loved the most. When speaking with her in an interview, the passion comes out naturally. Including it in her Passion Statement lets managers know she understands exactly what is important about this job.

Final sentence: "once committed to a project, there is nothing that can stand in the way of my success." The closing sentence is all about a key personality trait. Personality matters on resumes, not just facts. By demonstrating a relevant personality feature, it ties together all of the elements in the Passion Statement.

Using Passion Statements beyond the resume

A well-crafted Passion Statement can be used anywhere. It can be the basis of your networking introduction. You can use it in your

LinkedIn profile or other social media platforms. You can even use pieces of it in your cover letters.

Passion Statements are the one piece of your resume that is all about you - and that makes it a valuable tool throughout your job search process.

* * *

Guide their minds with logic trains

A great way to convey critical information in a short amount of time is to create logic trains. Logic trains arrange information in, well, a logical order. This means that each sentence logically leads to the next thought.

The simplest example of a logic train is listing your work experience in chronological order. The reader doesn't have to bounce back and forth between the jobs, trying to figure out the real order. In this aspect, the reader absorbs the information correctly because they don't have the guess or assume the meaning.

Arranging duties for a position with logic train is the next structure. For example, if you are describing your functions with leading a group of ten technicians, it would be logical to list the results afterwards. The same is true for awards and recognition: if it can be tied to the job instead of randomly inserted later, it creates extra value because the reader does not have to search for the related functions.

Skill sets contain logic trains as well. It would be highly unusual to list two computer skills, followed by staff management and then to jump back to more computer abilities. The reader is more likely to miss the relevance of a skill when they are not listed in logical order. One trick is to create two skill sets, one labeled "Technical Skills" and the other as "Personal Assets." The Technical Skills are all of the computer proficiencies, equipment, and so on. Personal Assets are the personality traits, such as "team player" or "highly motivated." These two sections create their own logic trains.

A well-crafted logic train helps the reader with comprehension, especially in the 30-second reading. If they don't mentally have to switch gears because you just switched subject matter, they can not only read faster, but actually gain some understanding.

Logic trains can be used in any resume format. Put some thought in what you are trying to say and the logic trains will appear naturally.

Getting to the essentials

The best resumes get to the point, no matter what style you use. Make it clear, concise and direct. Each sentence should contain one clear thought. Overly complicated or long sentences are more difficult for the reader to understand quickly. If you think a sentence is too long, say it out loud. If you can't finish it without taking a breath, it has too many words.

Look at this example – read it out loud. How does it sound to you?

Figure 5.2 Revising complex statements

Original -
Sentences are too wordy and too long

PROFESSIONAL EXPERIENCE

Operations / Customer Service Director
The Culture Promotion Company, Anytown, USA, 1999 – present
Demonstrated longevity in city and national entertainments, and promotional markets through reliable and consistent high quality presentations and supportive customer relations. Recipient of state and federal cultural awards. Coordinate, plan, promote and implement projects, parties and cultural events for family, K-12, disadvantaged and challenged communities. Curriculum development and delivery.

Revision -
Sentences are concise and simple, with a logical progression

PROFESSIONAL EXPERIENCE

Operations / Customer Service Director
The Culture Promotion Company, Anytown, USA, 1999 – present
Develops and delivers high-quality presentations, parties and cultural events for families, students and challenged communities. Provide dedicated customer service. Work closely with local and national entertainment and promotional markets.
- Recipient of state and federal cultural awards, 1992 and 1994

Notice how sentences in the revision are short and to the point. There is not more than one idea per sentence. The duties are easier to understand. By making the awards a separate indentation, they are emphasized more. Hiring managers like to see results, such as cost savings or awards. Look for ways you can add these to your resume, especially if they can be associated with a specific position.

Another common mistake is using the exact wording from the job description when describing a past job. This makes very boring and long-winded resumes. The only parts that need to be verbatim from the job description are the key terms in the skill set. Using the language from the job description to depict your experience will not win over a hiring manager. Feel free to paraphrase, while still capturing the relevance for the new job you want to have.

Dangers of falling in love
Ever had a job that you absolutely loved? Or something so unique that you feel it needs a complete description for employers to understand?

If this unique job is no longer your target, you need to be careful. Employers don't want all the details if it doesn't relate to their needs. If you're going on and on about a job you loved, you're telling the reader how much you want that job again.

In my own past, I was a radio morning show producer – an unusual job that not many people outside of broadcasting understand. Thinking I needed to educate people, here's what I wrote on my resume:

Figure 5.3: Dangers of falling in love with a job
Original -
Saying too much about a job indicates emphasis and passion... which can be a problem if this is not the target job.

MORNING SHOW PRODUCER, KXYZ-FM, Denver, CO
8/98 – 7/99
Prepared the studio daily; pulled and returned all spots and music; arranged guests, edited interviews in various computer, digital and analog media; researched news articles in print and electronic media; prepared sound effects and filler material; ran the audio board; maintained adherence to strict schedules; insured all contests conducts to legal and FCC standards; maintained archives in written, analog and digital tape formats; answered studio telephone lines; arranged travel itineraries; assisted with creative decisions; and made coffee.

Revision -
Simplify duties so that others in a different industry can understand the transferable skills...

MORNING SHOW PRODUCER, KXYZ-FM, Denver, CO
8/98 – 7/99
Intense multi-tasking, administrative, editorial, creative and supervisory position.
- Enforced adherence to strict schedules.
- Created and maintained a filing system for a variety of media.
- Managed a team of highly unique individuals.

What was the message I was sending to potential employers? That I loved this job and wanted something like it again! That was not the case at all. I was actually getting out of broadcasting, but nobody believed it from looking at my resume.

Giving it some more thought and doing more research into what employers were looking for led me to this revision.

The revised description gets to the heart of the job. With these changes, my number of interviews went up significantly because my resume's message was clear.

Stay on target
Brainstorm on these questions to find the gold for your resume: What are the essential components for your target job? Take the time to write several possible answers and then evaluate the answers.

How does this tie with your past experience? If you aren't sure what matters most, read your Key Element Detector again. Your personal values may be different from what the employers' need.

- **My main area of responsibility was:**
- **I spent most of my time doing:**
- **Things I handled that were not part of my job description:**
- **I am most proud of:**
- **I was recognized for:**
- **I would love to do this more:**

Achievements and scope

Look at your achievements. Is there something you can pull into your resume? Remember, hiring managers like results and successes listed in the resume. If you're having trouble thinking of accomplishments, include numbers to describe your past work - quantify it. For example, talk about how many clients you managed, the size of the company's revenue, how many people you managed, how many invoices you processed each week, and so on.

If you find areas you want to improve, do something about it. Take a class, complete an online tutorial, use training from your local Work Force Office - anything to fill that hole. Thanks to your Key Element Detector, you know what you need to add. Make yourself more attractive to employers and round out your abilities.

How about those duties you hated? Are they inevitable for your target job? If these are the Key Elements for a job, find a way to get over your own objections. Are they an opportunity for personal growth? Can you find something positive about the experience? If not, you might consider changing your target job to something you would enjoy more.

* * *

Feeling too thin?

Some resumes do not say enough - they are too thin. Nobody likes to read an overblown resume. However, employers must be able to gauge your experience or you will get rejected. They don't have time to play guessing games.

Never let HR assume what you did in a past job based just on the title. You would be surprised by the pre-conceived notions employers use to judge candidates.

Of course you understand what you did in your past job - but you need to make sure it is crystal clear to potential employers, too. It is up to you to make your experience relevant to the job you are seeking and phrase it in a way the employer can understand. This starts with having respect for your own work history and conveying that with the proper wording. Confidence does come across in your writing when you resume is balanced and professional.

Look at this example. Even when applying for internal jobs, this candidate never got an interview. Why? He was assuming the other employees understood his job as a Telephone Outreach Coordinator – the telemarketing group for a non-profit association. Even internally, management associated the division as "those telemarketers," hardly a position valued by many managers.

Figure 5.4: Expanding thin resumes

Original - Thin resume

JH CLIENT
303.555.1212   bogusemail@yahoo.com

Objective
To establish a successful professional career by offering business and service skills to help organizations achieve their goals.

Experience
Big CO– Telephone Outreach Representative – 10/2003-Present
Responsibilities include contacting donors to secure donations for auction events, servicing donors with follow-up information and fulfillment arrangements. Part-time: $xxx/hour + commission

No Name University – Telephone Fundraiser – 12/2003-5/2004
Part-time: $xx/hour + commission

Skills
Advanced computer technical abilities. Proficient in both Mac and PC computer environments.

Partial Revision of Thin Resume:

JH CLIENT
303.555.1212   bogusemail@yahoo.com

Skills
Proficient in both Mac and PC computer environments. Advanced in Microsoft Office, Excel, PowerPoint, Visual Basic, InDesign and Photoshop. Creation of WordPress websites. WAN and LAN network troubleshooting. Maintenance on printers, laptops, desktops and wireless network systems. Types 80wpm.

Experience
Big CO– Telephone Outreach Representative – 10/2003-Present
Conduct business-to-business calls for donations of goods and services. Contact members in regards to their membership and seek additional gifts. Resolve member problems and questions
- Successfully raised $XX,XXX for our annual televised auction
- Increased duties to include computer maintenance not only for the telephone outreach department, but also the executive branch.

When we revised his resume to show the reality of his experience and accomplishments, we expanded on the job description to explain what he was doing, in language hiring managers understand. Winning business-to-business donations is very different from calling little old ladies to get more money out of them - and that is what people thought he was doing. Adding accomplishments gets across the professional nature of the job. Notice how he included duties beyond his job description. Additional responsibilities will not be picked up by employers unless they are positioned correctly within your work experience.

Additionally, we moved his skill set to the beginning of the resume to give it more emphasis. Not many telemarketers have such extensive computer abilities. When these skills are highlighted, this candidate's value goes up. Soon after making these revisions, this candidate's invitations for interviews increased exponentially.

* * *

Assessing your value

Finding relevance is more than just searching key terms. Anyone can make a list of key words, however, that won't help you believe in your own worth as an employee. You have to determine your own value. Part of the process is giving yourself credit for your past accomplishments. Brainstorm answers for these questions to discover your own untapped value. While you may not use this information on your resume, it is important to develop self-recognition to increase your confidence.

- **In my last job, people didn't realize that I did:**
- **I have been recognized for:**
- **My co-workers say I can be counted on to:**
- **In my last job, I met this personal goal:**
- **What motivates me to do my best:**
- **To better myself, I learned to:**
- **I left this job because:**
- **In my ideal job, I would use this skill more:**

* * *

But I did the same thing in every job!

Do you feel that way about your work history? It may even be true... but it is the details that make the difference. Telling an employer about the scope of each job defines your abilities in a clear manner. Scope tells the employer how large or demanding a job was, giving a better picture of the unique nature of each past position.

If you had similar duties in your past jobs, pull out the details that made each position unique. How many clients did you help? What was your biggest task? Use measurable aspects of the job to describe the differences between them.

For example, in household management, it is the scope that defines the position. In private service, scope consists of the size of the home, the size of grounds, the number of staff members, the number of events in a given time period, and so on. Looked at individually, the jobs might seem to possess the same core responsibilities:

Figure 5.5 Adding details that matter

Original -
Without significant details, the most challenging job can look mundane...

Household Manager   2002 – 2011
Confidential Family - **Greenwich, CT**
- Provided housekeeping
- Prepared meals
- Helped with events
- Cleaned laundry

Revision -
With relevant details, the reader gets a sense of scope for the job...

Household Manager   2002 – 2011
Confidential Family - **Greenwich, CT**
Provided diligent management the principal's 20,000 sq ft home on 30 acres
- Supervised two housekeepers to meticulously clean all areas, with special attention to antiques, silver and fine artwork worth $7.5M
- Orchestrated extensive entertaining events for up to 100 guests on a monthly basis
- Prepared gourmet dinners 2-3 times per week
- Acted as ladies' valet, caring for high end designer clothing

You can apply this thinking to corporate jobs, too. Think of the variables involved in each of the positions. For example, there is a big difference between an HR department serving a company of 10,000 and a department looking after 20 employees. Same for sales; if your customer base demands a lot of attention, this is a very different job than looking after a high volume of low-maintenance clients.

Above all: Don't be boring

Use action verbs or descriptive statements to keep your resume interesting. Any sentence that starts with "demonstrated ability to…" should be stricken from your resume immediately. Don't stray into the area of fluff either – such as "lauded by many." Honestly, when have you ever seen the word "lauded" outside of Middle English poems you studied in high school English?

* * *

Final words on writing

Armed with a clear understanding of how to assemble your resume, you can go on to convey a very accurate message to any reader. Consider the emphasis you place on each section by its placement in the document and the volume you write about each piece. Items placed first carry the most emphasis. What you write about the most can say quite a bit about your passions.

If your resume is too fat, get to the essential parts that employers want. If your resume is too thin, pull in more value. Use your Key Element Detector to take the guesswork out and focus your presentation to achieve your goals.

Above all, do some work to determine your own worth. Showing respect for yourself is critical in any job search. Nobody will recognize your value as an employee until you can believe it yourself.

Chapter 6 - Opening Doors with Creative Cover Letters

No matter which route you use to apply for a job you will always need a cover letter. Even if you apply online, hunt for the option to include a cover letter. Even if Aunt Martha told you about the job with her best friend, you will send a cover letter. Did you meet someone through a networking event? Absolutely send a cover letter. Repeat after me: "I will always send a cover letter, no matter what!"

Why the big fuss? Because so many people fail to send cover letters at all, much less a relevant one. If you fail to send a cover letter, you lose a huge marketing opportunity. Even worse, you look like an amateur in the professional world because cover letters are a standard business practice. Ignore this unwritten rule and you will suffer the consequences. And the tougher the competition, the more critical the cover letter becomes.

Don't be fooled if the job posting did not ask for a cover letter. This is a test. Show your understanding of the employment game and send the letter.

Never walk away from an opportunity to stand above the crowd.

Your custom marketing piece

Resumes are written to fit the *type* of job; cover letters are customized to the *specific job*. Enhance your presentation by drawing attention to different skills, talents and experience on your resume. You can even introduce new information in the cover letter.

Employers want to hire people who are excited about their opportunity. Show your passion for their industry and their company in the cover letter. If you really want to stand above the masses, go to the company's website before you apply. Find something you relate to, a specific niche you fill or a way you fit their needs. Taking the few moments necessary to customize your cover letter can make the difference between an interview and a silent phone.

Understanding the basics

Cover letters are very short and targeted marketing pieces. They must be written in proper business format and follow business etiquette.

A Great Truth

Even though cover letters are formal business communications, it is still acceptable to let some of your personality through. After all, we are hiring people, not robots.

Always follow these general rules:

- *Never* write a cover letter that is longer than one page.
- Use proper business formatting, even in email.
- Name the job and state where you saw it advertised.
- Include your contact information: name, address, phone numbers, and email.
- Mention the best time to contact you, especially if you are in a confidential search.

For effectiveness, try using a couple of these tactics:

- Start with an interesting introduction.
- Find two or three key points in the job description and explain how you meet those requirements.
- Point out highlights in your resume.
- Be sure to tell them how your experience is relevant to their needs.
- Show an understanding of their industry and /or their company.

Format

Unlike resumes, cover letters need to follow a set format. Always write a standard business letter, as outlined in Figure 6.1.

You can send your cover letter in the body of your email. In that case, the header of the email counts as the address block. However, be sure to include your email address with your phone number in the conclusion paragraph. Don't assume that your email address will show on the receiver's header. It is better to be redundant with contact information than to risk losing it.

Figure 6.1: Formal business letter format

Your Name
Your Address
Your Email Address
Phone Numbers

    (three blank lines)

Contact Name
Company Address OR
Via Email + list email address

(two blank lines)

Dear Mr. So-N-So:
    (one blank line)
Introduction paragraph – include title of the job and where you saw it
    (blank lines between paragraphs)

2nd & 3rd paragraph – two or three key points that show how you fit the position
    (blank lines between paragraphs)

Conclusion – Salary requirements, where to reach you, confidentiality issues

    (two blank lines)

Sincerely,

    (three blank lines)
Your name

Enc. *(Short for Enclosures; it is acceptable to list how many documents or pages are attached.)*

Online applications follow the same format. Copy and paste your Word document into the field, leaving blank lines between the paragraphs to give visual separation to the reader.

Many large commercial employment websites let you load up to five versions of your cover letter. When applying, you can edit and customize the chosen letter before you send it. When loading up your stock cover letters, use an "XXXXX" in all capitals to recognize any variable information, such as your salary range.

* * *

Do Your Research

Chapter 8 covers unadvertised jobs in detail and the critical nature of research. However, even taking ten minutes to read a company's website before you apply can make a huge difference. A quick perusal can reveal ways to target the company in your cover letter. Additionally, some job postings on employment websites are not legitimate. If you make a habit of visiting the actual employer's website before you apply, you can uncover possible scams.

A Great Truth

Every single employer wants to hire someone who is interested in his company and this particular job. Address your cover letter to each specific situation to make an impact on the hiring manager.

When drafting your cover letter, pay attention to what the company does. What is their focus? Do they have a mission statement? Employers want someone who supports the company's vision or mission statement. Write about how well you fit into their niche. As much as possible, show them you want *their job,* not just any old job.

Who are the top executives? Be sure to read their profiles on the website. Some companies include their contact information as well. Even if they don't, you can find the top executives through LinkedIn.com. More and more companies list their LinkedIn or Twitter profiles on their website. If so, it's a good bet that their executives have their own profiles, and you may be able to connect with them through mutual connections or groups.

Anytime you have an opportunity to send your resume directly to top executives with a company, do so. Be bold and send the president a targeted, customized, intelligent cover letter. Getting their attention can gain you an interview.

Even if you send your resume directly to the hiring manager, remember to copy the HR department. Depending on the company's structure, the HR department can have a lot of power over applicants, even the clever ones. Following their rules shows you can understand and follow written directions.

When scanning the employer's website, look at their other open positions. More than ever, companies are not advertising all of their open jobs on the large employment sites. Checking out the other open jobs could lead to another opportunity. However, there is more to this exercise than just scanning for open jobs; look for the trends. Do certain departments have several open positions? If you have talents in more than one area, your value goes up.

Work your research into your cover letter. Making this effort demonstrates your high interest level and attention to detail. Most applicants don't take the ten minutes to do the simplest research. Use every angle to gain an edge on your competition.

* * *

Interesting Introductions

Often times, the first few sentences in your cover letter will set the tone for everything. In truth, it can even determine if your resume will be read at all. Take a risk and start with an interesting introduction. This helps you stand out from the crowd while showing your creative nature - no matter what the job.

Professional does not mean boring. It is possible to cover the vital information and still be interesting - dare to think outside the box!

There are a number of interesting introductions...

Unusual metaphors

An unusual metaphor can definitely grab some attention. Rather than a stale opening, the idea is to surprise the reader with two concepts that normally don't mix. The trick is to catch the reader by surprise. For example, equating shirt shopping with choosing a good accountant is an unusual metaphor:

Notice how the introduction incorporated the facts while drawing in the reader. If you are in a creative field, such as marketing or even sales, using a unique approach demonstrates your abilities. Take any and every chance to prove your skills.

Figure 6.2: Unusual metaphor

Dear Sirs:

In this flooded job market, finding a good accountant can be as easy as picking out a new shirt at the mall. However, finding that perfect candidate who can balance sound accounting skills with an in-depth understanding of the broadcasting industry can be more challenging. That is more like having a tailor-made garment that fits to perfection. . I can offer this rare mix of skills. Please consider this as my formal application for your Staff Accountant position recently posted on www.fakejobsite.com.

In fact, I believe many aspects of my experience would serve your needs well. As you will note on my resume, I am very skilled with complex billing procedures, tight month-end close schedules and intricate journal entries.

Please contact me at 303-555-1212. I would love an opportunity to discuss putting my varied skills to your advantage.

Sincerely,

Diligent Applicant

Beyond the unusual opening, the rest of this cover letter follows the standard format. Highlight at least three key skills or duties that relate to their needs. Close with the normal contact information.

Strong statements
Another tactic is to showcase your abilities. Don't be shy. Be confident about your strengths. Bring them right to the forefront of your presentation and use them in your cover letter. There is a specific formula for the opening of this letter: an acknowledgement of the top skills (with the job posting worked in), followed by your own claim to meet those needs - coupled with the ability to back that up:

Figure 6.3: Strong statements

> Dear Sirs:
>
> I am certain that every candidate's resume that you have received for your Executive Assistant position listed on the Megajobs website is claiming to be highly organized and highly skilled. I am no different - but as you will see in reading over my attached resume, my experience supports my claims.
>
> My past eight years supporting top executives has provided me with unmatched experience in working with an eclectic mix of personalities. Additionally, my strong business skills would transfer well to your needs, especially my advanced rating in vital computer programs, such as Microsoft Office.
>
> Please review my attached resume and references, and contact me if you feel my skills could serve your needs. I can best be reached at _____ however, please keep in mind that my career search is confidential. Thank you for your consideration.

In this example, the soft skills as well as the hard skills are emphasized. Why? For executive assistants, both are important. This was, once again, discovered during the Key Element Detector™.

If it feels like you're going over the top, don't worry about it. To make the proper impact in 30 seconds, you have to come on strong. What seems like arrogance to your own eyes doesn't come through that way to the reader, especially when they only have about 30 seconds to read it. It takes strong claims to get through to an audience fast.

Question and answer
Another technique to try is posing a question and then giving the answer - which is you, of course. Like the Strong Claims, this requires a specific format: ask the question, answer the question and then tell them how you possess that ability or experience essential to the job:

Figure 6.4: Question and answer

Dear Mr. Smith:

What could possibly be the single greatest asset of any sales professional? The ability to understand their clients' needs and help them come up with marketable solutions would have to rank pretty high – I know it certainly did in my past ten years of dedicated sales experience.

In fact, I believe many aspects of my experience would serve your needs for a _____ extremely well. As an Outside Sales Consultant for So-N-So Company, my sales were consistently above set goals, especially with my returning customers. I love every aspect of making the sale, from setting the initial appointment to closing the deal.

Combine this with my natural tenacity and drive, and you have a Sales Associate who not only delivers the numbers, but also has a real understanding of your clients' needs.

Please contact me at _____ as soon as is convenient for you. I would love for an opportunity to discuss putting my varied skills to your advantage.

Sincerely,

Sales Applicant

Paragraph 2 starts with the proof of your answer. It must relate back to a specific part of your resume, or this cover letter won't work. Paragraph 3 is your "bonus round," pointing out a personality trait that explains why you would be great for this job. This cover letter can be seen as a bold move by some, but in truth, it's another way of showing your understanding of the employer's industry and their needs.

The Most Powerful Cover Letter Ever

Of all the cover letters, showing a deep understanding the industry is the most powerful tactic. It also takes the most work. If you don't know the industry, or if you are just guessing about the facts, this type of cover letter won't work.

More than just a clever opening, understanding the industry shows a level of analysis in current economic conditions or industry turning points. To do this, you must stay in touch with your industry and use your knowledge and experience to your advantage. This means a lot of extra research, including trade magazines, local business newspapers, traditional newspapers, the company's press releases and even the important bloggers in your field.

These cover letters are also used for a hidden job market, that being any job that is not formally advertised. Since the job isn't even posted, you are actually pointing out that the manager needs you based on some current news or event. Trigger events can be anything from the company winning a large contract to a governmental regulation change. Even the manager's promotion could be a reason to pitch him or her for a job.

This sample cover letter is a real example that I used when I was still looking for work in the broadcasting industry (about a thousand years ago). There was no job advertised, but there was a large article in a local entertainment magazine which featured this conglomerate, as they had just purchased a chain of radio stations in the Colorado Mountains. Knowing that they would need to increase their staff, I sent a targeted cover letter and strong resume. Then I went on vacation. When I got back two weeks later, the president of the company had left three voice mails and one email to set up an interview with me. (See? It was so long ago, I didn't have a cell phone much less a smart phone...) The result was a series of three interviews with the top C-level executives at the company. A month later when the job was officially posted, it was based on everything I had to offer. Unfortunately, in the end, they hired a relative - but that's ok, because within 6 months they were off the air. Some things happen for a reason!

One of the big keys in this letter is the reference to the 1996 Telecommunications Act[1]. Anyone involved in radio understood exactly what that meant. It changed the face of broadcasting forever, and not always for the best. The fact that I understood the implications too meant tons – and gave me huge credibility.

Figure 6.5: Understanding the industry

Dear Mr. Smith:

After reading several articles about you and your company, I have become increasingly impressed. Specifically, I understand your vision to bring local radio back to being exactly that – local radio.

When I worked for Mega Huge Broadcasting, I moved through the ranks of the business office to the position of Morning Show Producer because of my belief in the company and our talent. Once there, I became disillusioned like so many of us have after the fallout from the 1996 Telecommunications Act. More recently, I have been working in the Finance Department of the Local TV station, rebuilding my vision of what is worth my loyalty and dedication. After learning of your own vision for your company, it sparked my reason for getting into radio – to serve the audience.

I would like to offer you my services. I am truly multi-skilled, as you can see in my attached resume. I offer you the use of my skills wherever you need them most.

I can be reached at _____. I look forward to speaking with you.

Sincerely,
Relevant Applicant

---

[1] The 1996 Telecommunications Act changed the amount of radio stations one company could own in a geographic market, defined by 1) number of stations and 2) percentage of market share. This caused numerous mergers and acquisitions, leading to mega-broadcasters who could control up to 30% of a local market. End result? Layoffs, loss of variety on the airwaves and a difficult market for new companies. In this sample cover letter, the writer is addressing an independent broadcasting company, trying to compete with huge companies in a major market.

If you really understand your industry, show off your knowledge. It will truly open doors that you didn't even know existed.

* * *

What *Not* To Do
Don't make these common mistakes...

Giving your life story
No matter what, don't go on too long or give your life story. This is different than the personal information shared in the powerful cover letter. Instead, it is a long, rambling, arduous accounting about every detail in your life. Recruiters and managers don't care. Even if your entire life has prepared you for this job, they won't read it. Any recruiter or hiring manager would dread such a rambling cover letter.

Figure 6.7: A life story

Dear Ms. So-N-So:

I am writing to you in regards to the Production Assistant position listed on the Megajob website. I have always had an extreme interest in television, and I believe I am the best candidate for this position.

I have significant experience and training in the broadcasting field. Even as a child, I would make home videos and edit them myself. My whole family could not recognize me without a camera in my hand. I took it upon myself to record every significant event in our lives. For fun, I would write short movies and get my friends to act in them. Needless to say, it wasn't Oscar-worthy material, but it gave me great experience.

As for my training, I graduated with a bunch of honors from Yakety University, with a Bachelors Degree in Communications. While in school, I did a bunch of both fictional and non-fiction pieces. I liked the journalism style the best, getting the images to match the reporter's story became my ultimate goal. While tracking down all these stories, I got a lot of experience with all kinds of equipment, from the various cameras to both digital and analog edit bays. But most significantly, I came to realize that my dreams of becoming a great asset to any studio or broadcast station could actually become a reality. .

Soon after my graduation, I gained a position doing camera work for Such-And-Such Studios. I proved my worth over and over by creating the best production pieces possible. We worked with businesses to create their commercials, but when times were lean, I was not above taping a wedding or two for the extra cash. As you can see, just like my family discovered, I'm best recognized with a camera in my hand. I think the wedding work actually became crucial to me, because it taught me how to listen to a client and give her the best possible video of her special day. I'm sure you can appreciate my accomplishments there!

In my most recent position at Blah Blah Studios, I moved up the ladder to become the top production assistant. Now more than just a superior cameraman, I can oversee an entire project and bring about the image the director is trying to convey. We haven't won any awards for our commercials yet, but we have been nominated! Best of all, I've gotten a lot of experience with incorporating graphic elements to the video we capture. This is something I would love to learn more. I am always looking to build upon my current skills.

As you will note on my detailed resume, I am wonderful and very qualified. Of course, any company will benefit from my experience! I look forward to meeting you at my interview.

Sincerely,
Joe Schmoe

Victim mentality

You may be the victim of budget cuts, layoffs or changes in your industry. Keep your wounded pride to yourself. Nobody is going to give you some slack because your job suddenly disappeared. In fact, writing about it in the cover letter makes employers uncomfortable and suspicious. Focus on what you have to offer the employer, rather than dwelling in the past. It will strengthen your presentation and your self-esteem at the same time.

Figure 6.7: Victim mentality

Dear Sirs:

I am very interested in your project coordinator position.

Recently, I was the victim of wide layoffs at my former company. Even though I had many talents that served the company well, they were forced to let me go due to financial difficulties. This was no reflection on my abilities, but merely forces beyond my control.

As you will note on my resume, I bring many skills to the table and I will work hard for you.

Thank you for your time,

Lame Applicant

Generic statements

A generic cover letter is better than nothing at all, but not by much. When you send something vague, you miss a marketing opportunity. You may have some stock cover letters that you use over and over, but keep them interesting. At the very minimum, your letter needs to address the industry or the vital elements of your job. Again, use your Key Element Detector™ to hone in on those important terms.

Figure 6.8: Generic statements

> Dear Sirs:
>
> I wish to apply for your Executive Assistant position recently listed online.
>
> As you will note, I have several years experience doing this type of work. I have always been reliable and loyal. While I have enjoyed my current job, I am seeking a new and challenging position in a stable company.
>
> Please call me as soon as possible to schedule an interview. I look forward to meeting you.
>
> Sincerely:
>
> Simple Applicant

Getting too casual

A properly written cover letter starts with the person's name, in the formal tense such as Mr. Smith or Ms. Jones. If you don't have a name, "Dear Sir" is acceptable. Never start with "Hi There," "Howdy," or any other cute term. It comes across as very immature and can even be taken as an insult.

Figure 6.9: Getting too casual

> Hello George!
>
> I am very excited to see your opening for a marketing manager. I just know that you could use an enthusiastic and talented person such as myself.
>
> My specialties are internet marketing, public relations and project coordination. As you can tell on my resume, I have always been involved in marketing, in various different aspects. I'm just sure you can use me in a number of different ways.

I will call you later this week to schedule an interview. I look forward to meeting you.

Sincerely,

Creepy Applicant

Grammar, verbiage and spelling

If your resume indicates that you have "excellent communication skills and attention to detail," your cover letter will be evaluated as proof of those claims. Grammar and spelling are crucial in the cover letter. It is better to have a simple, well-written cover letter than something thrown together quickly. Write your cover letter in Word first, run a good spell-check and then copy and paste the words into your email.

Dear Mr smith:

I am very interested in yourr position for an executive Assistant. If you are looking for a right-hand persona with excellent communication skills and great attention to details, I'm you're candidate.

Certainly anyone who claims to be detail-oriented and then leaves errors in his cover letter is not great with details.

* * *

Final words on cover letters

Strangely enough, most employers will read your cover letter after the resume. Your cover letter needs to enhance the resume, and especially tie back to why you want their job. Take the time to make your cover letter relevant, personal and interesting. Your ultimate message is how you understand their needs and how you fill that need. Convey this message and you will to rise to the top of the candidate pool.

Chapter 7 – Dealing with Discrepancies

You may have less-than-ideal situations in your past or current employment situations. How do you deal with issues such as gaps in your employment, switching fields or a lack of experience?

The first thing to change is your attitude. Conducting an empowered job search means reconciling your feelings about the past. Don't ignore an issue and then hope it won't be addressed in the interview. If you acknowledge the stumbling blocks, you can deal with them in an effective way. You have to accept a situation before you can solve it.

HR people are trained to spot the discrepancies in a resume. However, that does not mean a ripple in your experience will kill your chances. It is possible to get HR and hiring managers beyond the knee-jerk reaction of cutting any candidate that has a less-than-perfect work history. To do that, you need to look at the problem from the employers' point of view. What are their objections or concerns? If you can address the objection right from the start, you can move past it.

Three Steps to Reframing a Discrepancy
Every situation can be dealt with, if you have the courage to face it. To reframe a problem, follow these crucial steps:

1. **Honestly state what the issue is**

2. **Consider it from the employer's point-of-view**

3. **Discover the positive in the situation**

To reframe a discrepancy, take a moment to write down what you think may be holding you back. Be honest and thorough, writing down what the real issue is. Some possible problems could be a spotty work history, breaking into a new industry or even leaving a distressed industry (like mortgages).

Next, think of this problem from the employer's point-of-view. An unstable work history makes them nervous that you will not stay for a long term job. Switching industries has a number of risks; can they afford to take a chance on you? Even when they intellectually recognize a distress industry such as mortgages, there is a doubt in the back on their mind: is that really why you left a job?

Finally, think about how the event could be considered a positive. Write down your answer to those objections. It needs to be clear, specific and positive. For example, short-term jobs help you adapt quickly to new situations. Breaking into an industry means you are highly motivated to make a good impression on the job, not to mention bringing new ideas to the table. Leaving a troublesome industry is a smart move, plus you come to the table with transferable skills.

Sometimes the answer will require more work on your part. Did your Key Element Detector™ reveal some skills you are missing? Or a required education level? Now is a perfect time to take some classes. Since you've done your research, you know exactly what you need. Taking classes or workshops relating to your career shows your commitment to the job.

Don't wait around for someone else to solve your problem. Employers rarely stick their neck out for candidates anymore. However, when you are realistic about your own strengths and weaknesses, you become a confident candidate - and a real commodity in the job market.

Figure 7.1 Transforming discrepancies

The Issue	Employer's objections	The Positive Solution

Attitude is a major factor in the job searching process. It affects confidence levels, which employers can sense on a resume or in the interview. There is a noticeable difference between confidence and hiding something, even on the resume.

A Great Truth

Your resume is a marketing tool. The purpose is to get you the interview, not disclose everything about you. While you can't lie, you can use various techniques to convey a specific message.

Using temporary agencies effectively

Registering with various temporary agencies might be a viable solution, especially if you have been out of work for a while. Temporary work is a great way to discover the work environment you really want, while still earning some money.

Agencies always hire a large volume of employees. If you show up when you say you will, you've won half the battle. Reliability and availability are the two top attributes. Most agencies keep a large database of potential employees.

Many agencies let you do the tutorials on their computers. By updating your skills, you become a more marketable commodity. Similarly, as you prove your reliability, you will get more jobs. This can evolve into a permanent or long-term position.

Temporary work can help fill in gaps on your resume. In your Work History, you can list the entire time that you have been registered with an agency, even if there are small breaks in between the assignments.

Keep in mind that the temporary employee market is extremely competitive. You can register with more than one agency to increase the frequency of assignments. Temporary agencies are a great way to practice your follow-through skills. Take the initiative and call every Tuesday or Wednesday to ask about upcoming assignments; Monday is the worst day to call; they are usually too busy. Be willing to take a variety of jobs. Practicing willingness, professionalism and reliability keeps you positive in your overall job search.

An agency should not demand a fee from you

If an agency requires you to pay them for their services, be very wary. Most agencies get paid by the employers, not the candidates. If your recruiter is demanding a large fee up front, take a serious look at their track record and online reputation. Weight your options before you give them anything. What is included in their services? Are these tools you lack in your own job search? Offering to write your resume and to make some phone calls is not enough to demand a fee over $2,000. If you do need professional resume help, a reasonable fee is anywhere from $200 to $800, depending on your career level and experience.

* * *

Techniques for Specific Discrepancies

To effectively deal with any and all of these discrepancies, you must recognize the problem is *from the Employer's point of view.* This is another version of catering your resume to the employer's needs.

Returning to the work force

Perception Problem: Your skills are not up-to-date; unsure if you are serious about your job search; will take time for you to get up to speed.

Ways to overcome the perception:

Be confident and clear with your own personal goals and reasons for returning to work. Take some classes to update your skills. Be positive about your past work experience and find the relevance for new directions. Adding some volunteer activities, part time or temporary work while you are searching shows commitment to the work force.

Tips for your Resume & Cover Letter:

A strong Summary or Profile can bring instant recognition of your strengths and motives. Emphasize your skill set. Be sure to include any new classes or seminars you may have taken that relate to your career field.

In the following Sample Cover Letter, the Candidate directly addresses the employment gap, and uses it to her advantage. She shows how this time allowed her to realize the direction of her career. Not only that, she brings in her recent, self-directed education to fill in the gaps in her skill set.

Samples Follow...

Figure 7.2: Cover letter and resume for Returning to the Work Force

Candidate Returning to Workforce

Address - Phone - email

Dear Hiring Manager:

I understand how challenging it can be to find just the right mix of skills, experience and temperament for your Human Resources department. You need someone who not only understands the crucial regulations in the field, but also the important human element to the job. Best of all, you need someone who understands that well-served employees are more productive – and that affects your company's bottom line. Throughout my HR experience, I have understood these principles.

As you will note on my resume, I do have experience in a large corporate setting, overseeing the HR functions for over 3,000 employees. What might not be obvious is why I am interested in your assistant-level work.

> I am a hard-working and dedicated Human Resources professional who has been out of the market for a while. Currently, I am studying for my PHR certification test. I realize that you need someone with solid skills and knowledge – it is my goal to join a company in a junior role and work my way up in the department as my education becomes more complete.

This is the "kicker" paragraph that addresses the Objection

> Above all things, I am a team player. I believe in giving the best of myself, no matter what the role may be. This makes me an ideal HR Assistant. Combine these traits with my natural abilities in mentorship, communication, problem-solving and attention to detail and you have an ideal addition to your department.

This is further proof of the willingness to adapt

I look forward to hearing from you. I am seeking a salary between $XX,XXX and XX,XXX, which is in line with current salaries in the industry. I can be reached at _____.

Sincerely,

Candidate Name

Candidate Returning to Workforce

Address - Phone - email

HUMAN RESOURCES PROFESSIONAL

Dedicated HR professional with 10+ years of experience in large organizations. Supportive team player who is willing to help in any aspect to make sure the company reaches their objectives while remembering the crucial human element.

CORE COMPETENCIES:

- Proven attention to detail
- Benefits Coordination
- Recruitment, training and onboarding
- Federal, State regulation knowledge

- Adaptable Team Player
- Employee Event Planning
- Employee Recognition Programs
- Background checks and investigations

Technical Skills: Microsoft Office (Word, Excel, PowerPoint), data entry, file management

PROFESSIONAL EXPERIENCE:

Employee Relations Manager	**1997 to 2005**
Human Resources Generalist	**1993 to 1997**

Large Company, Anytown, USA

As the **Employee Relations Manager**, was responsible for 3500 employees (all levels—VP, Director, Management and Floor Personnel) and Environmental Services:

- Recruited, interviewed, hired, and conducted background checks for new personnel
- Conducted employee reviews and evaluations in accordance with EEOC/FMLA/ADA
- Investigated Grievances and Disputes: hostile environment, harassment, terminations
- Created training plans for performance improvement and career advancement
- Resolved personnel issues and implemented Employee Assistance Programs (EAP)
- Planned employee recognition events and managed retention programs
- Extensive documentation and accurate record-keeping for all personnel issues, including terminations, investigations and payroll records

EDUCATION, TRAINING AND PROFESSIONAL ASSOCIATIONS:

1993	**Bachelor of Arts,** University of Colorado
2010 - Present	Society for Human Resources Management (SHRM)
2010 - Present	Colorado Human Resources Association (CHRA)

PHR certification pending, 2011

2010 Professional Development Courses:
Compensation for HR Generalist, ER/ Diversity, Driving Engagement and Shaping Culture through Performance Management

Gaps in employment / long unemployment
Perception Problem: Why did it take so long to find your next job?

<u>Ways to overcome the Perception:</u>
Be sure not to blame any others. Remain positive when contacting potential employers, no matter how you feel. Be ready to explain these gaps in an interview –you will be asked, but there is no need to dwell on them.

<u>Tips for your Resume & Cover Letter:</u>
If you are coming from a field which suffered because of various economic factors, it is acceptable to remind others.

> *For example: In 2000, the IT industry crashed and has never been the same since. Many IT people were out of work for up to two years. Several people were forced into other industries or had to take positions below their skill level just to survive. As a result, their resumes frequently show major gaps in employment around 2000-2003. A gentle reminder of the economic climate at that time can help a recruiter understand the challenges that faced an entire industry.*

In some situations, you might want to put an explanation on your resume for the gap, but it must be handled with tact. No whining! If you must give an explanation, keep it positive and personal. If you needed to take some time for personal reasons, you may want to list it with statements such as "Personal Sabbatical" or "Personal time to assist older family member." It is not necessary to list a reason for a gap, but if you can do so with a positive spin, it can help get past a screener.

<u>A possible solution: acting as a consultant or contractor</u>
One solution that many professionals use for a long period of unemployment is to call themselves a "consultant." It is important to actually have some clients during this period to support your claim of working independently.

Volunteer experience is also important during periods of unemployment. It shows that you are still engaged in life, getting out of the house and upholding regular obligations. When volunteer experience goes back further than your gap, it is even more valuable.

For both Gaps in Employment and Returning to the Work Force situations: Emphasize your skills – especially as they pertain to your industry!

Samples Follow...

Figure 7.3: Cover letter and resume for Gaps in Employment

GAPS IN EMPLOYMENT CANDIDATE

Phone - Email - Address

Dear Sirs:

> Vision. Integrity. Perseverance. I am sure these could be the qualities you seek in your Executive Assistant. Now couple these values with the proven ability to handle any situation with style and grace - seem like to much to ask for in an assistant? Yet I practiced all of these principals on a daily basis in my work as a contract assistant.

This letter starts with a strong value statement to deflect focus on the current unemployment.

I am very interested in offering my professional services as an Executive Assistant for your company and to you in particular. As you requested in the job listing on CareerBuilder.com, I am attaching my resume and references to this email.

I won't bog you down with the fine points in this cover letter, especially since my detailed resume is attached. However, I do want to stress my recent work as a contract Assistant.

> For me, it is critical that I make a difference from the first day on the job. I believe in asking questions and taking careful notes through training to make sure that I do not waste your time with redundant questions. I recently completed my certifications in Word Press and Outlook, and would be able to learn your software and systems very quickly.

This paragraph supports the value of contract work.

I can be reached by my cell phone, XXXX or via email, XXXXXXXX@yahoo.com. I am flexible in regards to salary issues. My target is between $XX,XXXX , although I would be interested to hear your desired salary range.

Thank you, and I look forward to hearing from you.

Sincerely,
Diligent Candidate

GAPS IN EMPLOYMENT CANDIDATE

Phone - Email - Address

SKILLED ADMINISTRATIVE PROFESSIONAL

Throughout my career, I have been recognized as the go-to person in the office, the one who knows the systems, procedures and the industry. Able to see key areas to streamline processes between departments, resulting in increased accuracy and reduced costs.

CORE COMPETENCIES

- 10+ years experience
- Report creation and customization
- Highly detail-oriented and organized
- Excellent communication skills
- Able to work independently

- Supportive team player
- Intelligent and adaptable
- Time-sensitive, strong sense of urgency
- Project organization and implementation
- Multi-task & high volume environments

Advanced rating in Microsoft Office, including Word, Excel, PowerPoint
Current certifications in FileMaker Pro, WordPress and Outlook

PROFESSIONAL EXPERIENCE

CONTRACT ADMINISTRATIVE ASSISTANT
Multiple Agencies including Sunny Side and Exemplar Staffing, Denver, CO   **2010 - Present**

Works a variety of assignments in offices throughout the Metro region.
Highlights of service include:
- Worked with accounting to follow up on invoice discrepancies
- Created templates to streamline extremely detailed policy data entry
- Developed mail merges and other automated tools for PR/ Marketing firm
- Created specific reports for Human Resources to track employees' performance

SENIOR ADMINISTRATIVE ASSISTANT
Small Business, Denver, CO   **2006 - 2009**

Provided key support to the 30-person office.
- Created and managed all account documentation for a $1.2 M book of business
- Submitted financial information for financing approval
- Worked closely with other departments to identify and resolve issues
- Conducted records processing, account documentation and claims documentation

VOLUNTEER EXPERIENCE

Denver Dumb Friend's League,   1996 - Present

Self-employed/ Being your own boss

Perception Problem: can you handle having a supervisor; will you insist on doing things your own way; are you comfortable working on a team?

<u>Ways to overcome the Perception:</u>

Be very clear that you enjoy working with a team. Understand your own motivation and be able to articulate it clearly. Show your willingness to be supervised or to lead.

Do your research on the company: while your reason for seeking a corporate job might be the benefits or security, don't let them know that! Instead, emphasize what you hope to gain from the new job: working with others, learning a new process, getting involved with an exciting product or service. Whatever it is, find a proper motive that relates directly to this company.

<u>Tips for your Resume & Cover Letter:</u>

Acknowledge your past success at the same time as stating your desire to move in a different direction. For example: "while I have enjoyed my career, I am looking forward to making a change and joining your team."

Do a comprehensive Key Element Detector™. Make sure to use the relevant key terms. One problem the self-employed face is disconnection from the current buzzwords. Plus, what was critical in your own business may not be the employer's top need.

On your Work History or in your Summary, write about times when you worked closely with others, or when you displayed leadership. Working with a variety of customers and adapting quickly to their style would transfer well to most corporate environments.

In your skills section, be sure to emphasize the softer skills associated with working in a team environment, such as "Excellent Communication Skills" or "Supportive Team Player." Look at the level of the position. What personality traits are essential for success? Show your aptitude in those areas. Back these statements up with clear examples in your cover letters or during interviews.

Samples Follow...

Figure 7.4 Cover letter and resume for Self-Employed

SELF-EMPLOYED CANDIDATE

ADDRESS - EMAIL - PHONE

Dear Sirs,

As a manager myself, I can appreciate the difficult task of hiring the right Sales Manager for the business. This is a decision that affects not only the Sales department, but the success of your entire business.

> Throughout my career, I have fostered the growth of our Sales Departments. More than just setting quotas and expecting results, I believe in training and mentoring new employees to gain the best results in the shortest time possible. Marketing is essential for getting potential business in the door, but it is the sales staff that provides the relationships which turn leads into clients.

This paragraph shows the understanding of the job and the skills required.

> Currently, I am seeking a position as the Sales Manager for your company. As you will note on my resume, I have spent the last several years developing sales teams for my own business. While I have enjoyed the success of running my own business, I look forward to mastering a new industry with the same diligent customer service that grew my company.

Followed by the desire to work with the company.

I look forward to speaking with you. I can be reached anytime at XXXXXX.

Sincerely,

Diligent Applicant

SELF-EMPLOYED CANDIDATE

ADDRESS - EMAIL - PHONE

DYNAMIC SALES MANAGER

For over 20 years, I have grown businesses through my willingness to work with others to reach shared goals. I believe in mentoring sales teams to achieve real growth through professional development. I encourage fostering long-term customer relationships to build repeat and referral business.

KEY ACHIEVEMENTS

- Grew company from a small start-up to annual revenues of $30M+
- Created ongoing client relationships, gaining a 80% referral rate for new clients
- Upheld high profit margins in a slow economy
- Recognized as top franchise for three consecutive years (2005 - 2008)

EXPERIENCE

CEO & SALES MANAGER   1995 - 2010
Dynamic Chrysler, Denver, CO
Franchised dealership with 50+ employees. Ranked as one of the top dealerships in US.

- Directly managed teams to achieve consistent growth in a competitive market
- Hired, trained and mentored junior sales associates
- Maintained financial controls for the business
- Created and executed multi-level marketing plans
- Worked with distribution for seasonal and national sales campaigns
- Set team and individual sales goals and quotas, adjusting performance as needed

CORE COMPETENCIES

- 10+ years of Sales Leadership
- 20+ years of Professional Sales
- Strategic Planning & Solutions
- Strong negotiation and closing ability
- Hiring and development of sales teams

- Excellent Communication Skills
- Diligent customer service
- Various CRM programs and reporting functions (ACT, Salesforce)
- Market research and development
- MS Office: Word, Excel and PowerPoint

EDUCATION

Bachelor of Science, Denver University, 1995

NOTES:

Unrelated work history/ multiple fields
Perception Problem: you're not serious; uncommitted to my field

<u>Ways to overcome the Perception:</u>
Emphasize your dedication to the new job. Tell them why you know this career is the right choice for you. Showing some real personal reflection makes you more believable. Be prepared to answer this in the interview as well – you need to be consistent at every point. Researching the specific company can also be very valuable - why do you want to work with these people?

<u>Tips for your Resume & Cover Letter:</u>
Tell them why you are drawn to this field. A strong Key Element Detector™ can show you the relevant duties and skills in your experience. If you are lacking a skill, take a class to become a more valuable employee. Paying for it yourself shows dedication.

If you have jobs in your past that are more relevant to your chosen field, you can emphasize that by two different Work History sections. One is the Relevant Experience; the other is the Additional Work History. Write less about the non-relevant experience.

Samples follow...

Figure 7.5: Cover letter and resume for Unrelated Work History

Unrelated Work History Candidate
Address ✦ phone ✦ email

Dear Sirs,

What could possibly be the greatest single asset for any private instructor? I know that the ability to adapt to the individual's learning style along with creating compelling curriculum would rank pretty high - I know it certainly did in my experience with the Salt Lake City School District.

> ➤ In fact, I believe that many aspects of my experience would serve your needs for an instructor very well. As a teacher, it was my goal to make the lessons memorable and fun - both crucial pieces for retention and adoption of the deeper meaning. Not only that, but my studies abroad has given me real-world experiences that the students can relate to.

This paragraph highlights how the experience directly relates to the hiring manager's need.

Combine this with my natural patience and compassion, and you have a private instructor who will adapt to the student's specific needs. It is this type of personal attention that creates lessons to last a lifetime.

Please feel free to contact me anytime at xxxx. I look forward to hearing from you.

Sincerely,

Diligent Applicant

Unrelated Work History Candidate
Address ✦ phone ✦ email

PRIVATE INSTRUCTOR
Providing dedicated, patient and compassionate instruction in foreign languages since 2004. I delight in helping adults, teens and children learn and gain appreciation in other cultures.

SKILLS SUMMARY

- 5+ years formal teaching experience
- 2+ years experience teaching English
- Company-trainer experience

- Fluency in foreign language and culture
- Organization of educational programs
- Curriculum development

EDUCATION

2008   Bachelor of Arts, University of Colorado - Denver, CO
Summa cum laude, Applied Linguistics

Fall 2000 Certification, Istituto Europeo - Florence, Italy
Studied vocal performance, Neapolitan folk music, Art History (Italian emersion course)

PROFESSIONAL EXPERIENCE

English Language Arts Teacher   01/2010 - Present
Salt Lake City School District, *Salt Lake City, UT*
- Plan and conduct novel lessons integrating modern classroom technologies
- Collaborates with fellow teachers to ensure students' cross-curricular development
- Prepare students for higher education and college entrance

Substitute Teacher   02/2008- 12/2009
Alpine School District, *Steamboat Springs, CO*
- Regularly requested by high school English, Math and Music teachers
- Instructed privately in languages and mathematics through post-secondary level

Private Language Instructor   12/2000 – 05/2003
Private Residence, Los Angeles, CA
- Coached novice student through to fluency in Italian
- Coordinated several multi-week cultural and linguistic excursions in Italy

ADDITIONAL EXPERIENCE

Administrative Assistant   12/2003 – 01/2008
Italian Embassy, Washington, DC
- Provided office support to foreign dignitaries

<u>NOTES:</u>

Unstable work history
Perception Problem: Is there something wrong with you- why do you change jobs so quickly or often? Lack of commitment.

Ways to overcome the Perception:
Show your commitment to this industry, and not just by writing about it. Increase your education through formal education, seminars or workshops. Conduct personal self-evaluation to your passion. Self-knowledge is the key!

Tips for your Resume & Cover Letter:
One way employers test your knowledge on your resume is the proper use of industry-related jargon. A complete Key Element Detector™ exercise will pinpoint the terminology unique to your industry. People who don't use jargon correctly will not be taken seriously.

Rather than list each individual job, which can look "choppy," create an employment summary. To be effective and honest, be sure to tell them on your resume that this is a summary. You will go over the specifics during an interview. De-emphasize jobs that have nothing to do with your chosen field. Remember, the things you write about the most shows your emphasis.

To really be effective, your cover letter should be very well researched, addressing the specific employer's needs. With an unstable work history, it is a serious uphill battle to get through the HR screening. This means you must get in touch with the hiring manager to make your case for hiring you. To do that, you must personalize your efforts. If you are unable to reach the hiring manager, your standard cover letter should address your passion for the field, or emphasis on your technical skills.

Samples follow...

Figure 7.6: Cover letter and resume for Unstable Work History

Unstable Work History Candidate
Address - Email - Phone

Dear Sirs,

> I recently read in Forbes that your company will be expanding in the Denver market in the next few months. I am sure that you are very busy with preparing for the change, but have you created a plan for your increased IT needs as well?

Even if the job is posted, it is critical to tie back to some recent news about this specific company. It will impress the hiring manager.

> Over the past few years, I worked contract positions which have prepared me to step into any situation and create a positive benefit. My clients have not only saved time and money, but they also decreased their down-time and increased productivity.

This is your benefit to the company

I am sending you my resume for your review. As you will note, I have experience with a wide variety of software, hardware and operating systems. Regardless of what systems you currently use, I am sure that I have experience with them.

> Most of all, I love creating solutions for a business's crucial IT needs. Whether it is planning the next system upgrade or squeezing another year out of current equipment, I believe in addressing the company's needs. I am here to help.

This is the passion statement, related back to the company's needs

Please feel free to contact me at xxxx. I look forward to hearing from you.

Sincerely,

Diligent Applicant

Unstable Work History Candidate
Address - Email - Phone

OVERVIEW OF QUALIFICATIONS
- 5 years of experience as IT Manager and System Administrator
- $950,000 in reduced cost savings through infrastructure and system management
- Contract management including Service Level Agreements and Managed Contractor
- Increased system uptime and reliability to over 99% utilizing ITIL v3 methodologies

WORK EXPERIENCE

June 2011 - Present
Senior System Administrator, BigCo, Denver, CO
- Provided technical support to users requiring email and security configuration
- Assisted with remote login configuration and access to network data systems
- Reconfigured user hardware to meet University access policies and standards
- Fielded general user queries concerning: connectivity, applications, access, and account status

From September 2007 to May 2011, accepted various contract and short-term assignments as a Consultant, Field Technician, and Field Services Engineer. Highlights of service include:
Field Technician, Some Service Group, Anywhere, USA 2011
- Specialized in troubleshooting various legacy hardware systems at the customer's location.

Field Service Engineer – XYZ America Inc, Denver, CO 2009- 2010
- Managed individual accounts and supported ongoing sales and service contracts
- Involved in project planning for new equipment installs

Contract Network Engineer, Server Operations Resolution Team -
Some Business Services Inc, Denver, CO 2007 & 2008
- Proposed solutions and fulfilled strict due diligence
- Analyzed services failures and anomalies to determine root cause

TECHNOLOGY

VMWare – Infrastructure 3	*OPERATING SYSTEMS:*
Symantec EndPoint Protection	Windows XP / Vista / 7
EMC Retrospect Backup	Windows Server 2003 / 2008
Nagios Infrastructure Monitoring	RedHat Enterprise Linux 5.4
WiseTrack Asset Management/Tracking	
Adobe Connect Pro – Web Conferencing	*CERTIFICATIONS:*
Symantec NetBackup	ITIL V3 Foundation Certification
Polycom Web Conferencing	VMWare Workstation 6 Certification

Overqualified/ too much experience
Perception Problem: you will get bored; you're only taking this while you search for a better job; you won't stay; I can't afford you.

Ways to overcome the Perception:
Be clear about your desired change and why. Clear motives are more believable to a future employer. Take a good look at your Focus exercises from Chapter 2.

Tips for your Resume & Cover Letter:
 Make sure the past duties listed relate to this new endeavor. Be honest, and make sure to state your motives in a tactful manner. No whining!
 You must do a complete Key Element Detector™ exercise to find the terminology unique to your industry. This will show you what to exclude and help overcome the impression that you are only doing this to "tide you over." It will be necessary to de-emphasize parts of your resume, so employers are not distracted about more demanding positions in your past.
 Another clue from your Key Element Detector™ is their desired years of experience. If the employer wants someone with 5 years of experience, and you list over 20, you are obviously overqualified. Instead, limit your resume to only the past 10 years of experience. In your summary, use "5+ years of experience..." This is technically true; 20 years is equal to 5+ years experience.
 Some people will call this "dumbing-down your resume." I prefer to call it targeting. You need to adjust your resume to what they are looking for to get the interview. Then you can prove your abilities and value when you meet the hiring managers face-to-face. BUT you won't get the opportunity if you make the mistake of appearing overqualified.

Ageism
Perception Problem: You're too old and set in your ways; I will have trouble training you; you're overqualified; you won't stay a long time; you want too much in salary

Ways to overcome the Perception:

Show eagerness and enthusiasm in your cover letter. Taking some classes to brush up skills on latest techniques shows your ability and willingness to learn. Be clear about your own goals and motivations.

Tips for your Resume & Cover Letter:
Do not list your entire work history. Only list the last 10-15 years of your experience. Don't include personal information in either your resume or cover letter. You can refrain from listing your college graduation date to limit guesses on your age.

Once again, you must do a complete Key Element Detector™ exercise research of the terminology unique to your industry. This way, you will highlight the skills and abilities that are currently in demand.

NOTE: Sample Figure 7.7: works for both Overqualified and Ageism...

* * *

Figure 7.7 Cover letter and resume for Overqualified Candidate

OVER QUALIFIED CANDIDATE

Address: Phone: • Email

Dear Sirs,

> I am certain that every candidate's resume that you have received for your Senior Sales Associate listed on Monster.com is claiming to be a great producer who provides top-notch customer service. I am no different; but as you will see in my attached resume, my experience supports my claims.

These statements set up an expectation of solid experience in the resume.

> For the past several years, I have been listed as the top salesperson in my region. When I first stepped into the role, a good deal of the existing clients were migrating to other carriers. To stop this flood, I reached out to every single customer in my territory, pro-actively discovering their problem areas and solving them before it drove the customer to leave.

This is a specific situation that applies to their needs.

Now, A good deal of my business comes from referrals of current clients. To my customers, I am known for my problem-solving skills. To my managers, I am known for my revenue-producing abilities.

I hope to provide both services to your company.

I look forward to speaking with you. I can be reached anytime at xxx.

Sincerely,

Diligent Applicant

OVER QUALIFIED CANDIDATE

Address: Phone: ▪ Email

DRIVEN SALES PROFESSIONAL

For over 10 years, I have exceeded both my personal and my professional sales goals. I live to find the clients, discover their needs, build the relationship and close the deal. Once committed to a project, there is nothing that can stand in the way of my success.

CORE COMPETENCIES

- 10+ years of Proven Sales Excellence
- Revenue and Profit Growth
- Proactive Customer Retention
- Accurate Forecasting and Pipeline Management

- Prospecting, Cold Calling and Networking
- Negotiating and Closing Expertise
- Communications Expert
- Solid Microsoft Office Skills

CAREER OVERVIEW

Telecom Company, Anytown, USA   1999-2011

National Wholesale Account Manager

During the early part of the century, Telecom aggressively pursued enhanced business services beyond their well-known wireless networks. Worked to promote these services to large enterprise customers.

- Sold layer 3 products such as Long Distance, Private Line, Internet, Web Hosting, Collocation
- Regularly interacted with clients on legal, finance, marketing and business analysis
- Coached and mentored newly hires that significantly reduced ramp time
- Served as member of the Vice President Advisory Board
    o Managed accounts that generated $36M revenue annually
    o Awarded with President's Club and 100% Club distinctions
    o Recognized as the #1 account manager in 2001

Regional Account Manager

- Managed retailed accounts, selling LD, Frame Relay, ATM, Internet, Collocation, Web Hosting
- Provided excellent customer service to existing clients
    o Highly regarded as the #1 account manager in 1999

EARLIER CAREER

BigCo, Anytown, USA

Major Account Manager | Regional Client Account Manager | Inbound/Outbound Sales

EDUCATION

Bachelor of Arts, Big University, Anytown, USA

PROFESSIONAL DEVELOPMENT

Situational Sales Negotiation | Managing for Impact | Power-Based Selling | World Class Selling

123

NOTES:

Underqualified/ lack of experience

Perception Problem: I'll have to teach you everything; you don't have the skills to do this job

Ways to overcome the Perception:
Realize your shortcomings and find a way around it. You may need to increase your education, either through formal schooling or workshops and seminars. Even without further education, less experience people are easier to train to do things their way. You need to convey how fast you can learn. Go the extra mile and put effort to reach key managers. Your ambition can overcome their doubts.

Tips for your Resume & Cover Letter:
In your cover letter, emphasize your interest in their position and your desire to learn more. Target the specific company in your cover letter.

Emphasize your skill set, and have a strongly written Summary or Profile. If you are a new college graduate, emphasize your education by adding more details, such as your major/ minor or any areas of special study. Be sure to include any new classes or seminars that relate to your career field.

You must do a complete Key Element Detector™ exercise to research of the terminology unique to your industry. Improper use of jargon is a huge screening tool to cut people with less experience.

Samples follow...

Figure 7.8: Cover letter and resume for Underqualified Candidate

Underqualified Candidate
Address - Email - Phone

Dear Sirs,

I am very interested in your Medical Assistant position listed on your website.

> I have always been passionate about helping others, especially in concerns to their health. As I was so interested in this industry, I recently received my diploma in Medical Assisting to start my new career.

This paragraph explains the passion and interest in the industry

Through my internship and in school, I learned the vital skills for this job. Even better, I learned how to harness my compassion for helping others with best practices in the medical field.

> In addition to my internship, I have been volunteering at the children's burn unit at Good Samaritan Hospital. It is so rewarding to help others in a difficult time in their lives. I hope to continue this good work while I expand my knowledge in this crucial field.

The passion is further supported by volunteer work

Thank you, and I hope to hear from you shortly. I can be reached at xxx.

Sincerely,

New Graduate

Underqualified Candidate
Address - Email - Phone

MEDICAL ASSISTANT

Years of customer service, effective communication skills, friendliness, and flexibility with adults and children. Self starter take initiative, quick learner a stable work ethic, integrity and honesty with a managerial background.

EDUCATION

Medical Assistant~ Diploma   **2011**
Community College, Local Source, USA

HIGHLIGHTS OF QUALIFICATIONS

➢ Customer Service attitude
➢ Compassionate, committed to helping others
➢ Assume responsibility to complete assignment
➢ Equally effective working alone or as a member of a team
➢ Dependable, hardworking, efficient and highly reliable
➢ Determined to excel, willing to take on new challenges and responsibilities

SKILLS AND ABILITIES

Blood Draws	Computer Applications	Laboratory Techniques
EKG	Record Keeping	Clinical Procedures
Physiology and Pathology	Accounting	Diagnostic Procedures
Medical Terminology	Coding	Pharmacology
Data Entry (50 wpm)	Insurance Processing	Medical Terminology

WORK EXPERIENCE

Medical Assistant Externship (160 Hours)   **2011**
Dialysis Distributor   **Anytown, USA**

Escorting the patients to treatment floor and take pre-treatment vitals. Performed glucose testing, blood draws and administered heparin. Set-up and took down dialysis equipment. Cleaned and sanitized dialysis machines between treatment sessions. Supplies restocked as needed. Patient vitals checked and data entrees every half hour.

Assistant Office Manager   **2008 - 2010**
Truck Company   **Anytown, USA**

Supervised up to 30 employees and maintained OSHA safety standards at all times. Opening and closing of the business, maintained client and vendor accounts. Organized schedules for drivers. Sales representative and customer service, accounts receivable, data entry and filing duties performed. Maintained and cleaned business office daily.

VOLUNTEER EXPERIENCE

9 News Health Fair	Bone Density Testing	April 2011
Good Samaritan Hospital	Children's Burn Ward	2010 - Present

<u>NOTES:</u>

Too long in one job

Perception Problem: you're set in your ways; difficult to adapt to a new situation; lack of ambition

<u>Ways to overcome the Perception:</u>
Continue to increase your knowledge. Show willingness to change, and an eagerness for a new opportunity. Be clear about the value of your experience – how does it relate to the employer's need?

Another problem with a stagnant career is lack of ambition. Don't make the mistake that people reward loyalty with promotions or new opportunities. They don't. They promote the people who are showing personal initiative to take on new duties, additional education or special training seminars. If your career is stalled, it is up to you to jump-start it. After all, your career is your responsibility. Once you make the first move, employers are more likely to believe your desire to change.

<u>Tips for your Resume & Cover Letter</u>:
Show increases in responsibility within in the job, or show ways you continued to perfect and refine what you did. Emphasize times when you adapted to new procedures, technologies or techniques. Add accomplishments to show progression in your career.

Once again, you must do a complete Key Element Detector™ exercise research of the terminology unique to your industry. This way, you will highlight the skills and abilities that are most current, keeping you relevant to the employer's needs.

Samples follow...

Figure 7.9: Cover letter and resume for Long Term Job Candidate

LONG TERM JOB CANDIDATE
Address - Email - Phone

Dear Sirs:

> I understand that you are seeking a new manager for your customer service department. Throughout my career, I have been dedicated to providing high-level dedicated customer advocacy, with special attention to detail and a sense of urgency.

> This letter uses the Passion Statement to set the tone for the letter and fight the apathy associated with long-term jobs

> During my time with International Company, I have continued to perfect my work and train others in the department. As a result, we have increased our efficiency, reduced errors, sped up delivery times and increased sales - all with less staff than before. Many of my ideas to streamline procedures directly impacted our ability to serve the customer better.

> Increasing responsibilities are highlighted here

> Currently, I am seeking my degree from Denver University to prepare me for management roles within an international company. Already, I have been using what I learned in the classroom in real-world application. With this new knowledge, I am certain that I am on the right career path. I look forward to helping others become better customer advocates through collaborative leadership.

> This shows current steps to further the career

> Currently, my salary requirements are XXXX. I can be reached at xxx, however, please keep in mind that my search is confidential.

> Salary requirements are crucial for a long-term job candidate -and must be in line with the industry

Sincerely,

Advancing Applicant

LONG TERM JOB CANDIDATE
Address - Email - Phone

LEAD CUSTOMER ADVOCATE

Throughout my career, I have used my gift for organization to bring order and efficiency through high level customer relationship management. By taking care of their daily needs, I solve problems before they endanger the long-term business. I believe in being responsive with a sense of urgency and attention to detail.

TECHNICAL SKILLS AND PERSONAL ASSETS

- 10+ years of support experience
- 5 years of project management
- Vendor management
- Flexible and dependable team player
- Strong problem-solving abilities
- Personally responsible and supportive
- Independent decision-maker
- Extremely detail-oriented

Intermediate to Advanced ratings on MS Office 2010: Project, Word, Excel, Power Point & Visio; Adobe Photoshop Element 10

PROFESSIONAL EXPERIENCE

International Company, Littleton, CO
January 1998 - Present
Since 1998 provides complex customer service in the roofing and insulation division.
POSITIONS OF INCREASING RESPONSIBILITY:

December 2005 - Present
Customer Lead Advocate, Retail Accounts Insulation Group
- Managed a territory of 10 Mountain and South Central states
  - Streamlined order processing to increase accuracy by 10%
  - Increased sales by 15% by proactively calls customers to seek additional orders
- Coordinates efforts with other team members
  - Works closely with 3 internal Pricing Representatives and 4 Outside Sales Representatives to insure proper information in bids, orders and proposals
  - Trains other Customer Advocates as needed

December 2000 - December 2005
Customer Advocate, National Accounts Insulation Group
- Directly responsible for over 300 Home Depot retail stores in an 8-state territory:
- Trained new employees on procedures for major accounts

January 1998 - November 2000
Guarantee Services Coordinator
- Issued guarantees and warrantees for Sales team, customers and contractors

EDUCATION
Bachelor of Arts, Denver University, Denver, CO
Planned graduation date: December 2012

<u>NOTES:</u>

Decreased salary expectations

Perception Problem: you're not serious about my job; you'll only stay here a short time while you look for "something better;" you can't afford to live on this salary

Ways to overcome the Perception:
Be clear about your motivations and goals. If you have re-arranged your personal situation to fit this lower salary, let them know - be honest - but without whining.

Tips for your Resume & Cover Letter:
In cover letter, be sure to mention your salary range. Tell them why you are excited about their specific opportunity, and why it fits in with your employment goals. Do some research on the company and use it in your cover letter. Your ambition can overcome their doubts.

On your resume, don't list non-relevant duties. If you're looking to make a switch, keep the duties targeted. (Key Element Detector™) Putting greater emphasis on your Skills could balance a thinner Work History.

Samples follow...

Figure 7.10: Cover letter and resume for Decreased Salary Expectations:

DECREASING SALARY CANDIDATE
Address - Email - Phone

Dear Sirs:

> ➤ I am very interested in your Office Manager position listed on craigslist.com.

| Be very clear about the job title |

> ➤ As I am sure you will note on my attached resume, I have several years of experience in business consulting and financial functions; what may not be as apparent is the support work I have done. You may even wonder why I would be interested in your position.

| This technique address the possible problem head-on, acknowledging the objection |

> ➤ The reason is simple: I love being the right-hand person in a busy office. Whether it is drafting documents, arranging travel or taking care of the mundane needs of the office, I get a great deal of personal satisfaction in supporting the company's vision. I am seeking a job where I can be the go-to person, the one you can rely on in any given situation.

| The answer is your Passion Statement: why do you want to do this? |

I have excellent computer skills, and I am detail-oriented, while not losing sight of the big picture. I am a creative problem solver who loves office work.

> ➤ Please feel free to contact me at xxxx if you have any questions. I am seeking a salary between $_____ , with flexibility regarding benefits. I would love for an opportunity to discuss putting my varied skills to your advantage.

| Salary requirements MUST be stated to be taken seriously |

Thank you,

Diligent Applicant

DECREASING SALARY CANDIDATE

Address - Email - Phone

OFFICE MANAGER SUMMARY

Throughout my career, I have provided support to those around me. I thrive on challenging situations, allowing me to shine while handling problems with grace. I am seeking my next great career: to help others through dedicated office management.

TECHNICAL ABILITIES:

Expert rating in Microsoft Excel and Outlook
Advanced skills in Microsoft Word
Comfortable with PowerPoint and various data base systems
Highly skilled in various accounting programs (QuickBooks, Peachtree, Great Plains)
Firm understanding of creating high-impact documents and presentations

WORK EXPERIENCE:

Senior Financial Analyst/ Business Planner
International Small Business   Los Angeles, CA   2007 to August 2011

- Worked closely with an international staff, requiring patience, understanding and adapting to widely diverse communication styles
- Developed effective procedures and tracking mechanisms, reducing errors and increasing comprehension between various departments
- Coordinate monthly, quarterly, and annual close processes Handled challenges of international computer interfaces on a daily basis
- Lead monthly account management meetings for executive staff
- Provide training and guidance to junior staff

Senior Consultant
Own Company   Los Angeles, CA   1996 to 2006
Personally operated small consulting company, offering business analyst services to various industries, such s health care, software development and manufacturing. List of Companies Available Upon Request
Duration of assignments ranged from 2 weeks to 9 months

- Provided traditional accounting and financial analyst services to clients
- Assessed situations, company needs and existing procedures to make effective suggestions

EDUCATION

Bachelor of Arts in Business Administration
Adams State College-Alamosa, Colorado 1990

<u>NOTES:</u>

Increased salary expectation

Perception problem: why are you worth this much; I can get the other candidate for less

<u>Ways to overcome the Perception:</u>
Prove your worth, stay within the acceptable range for this position and location. Commercial employment sites have resources for Salary Comparison, specific to the job descriptions, experience level and ZIP code. Researching a position's comparable salary is a legitimate negotiating tool.

> *For example, in the Denver area, Executive Assistants with 5-7 year of experience earn between $45,000-60,000. It is a reasonable expectation for someone trying to move into the Executive Assistance field to seek a beginning salary of $45,000 - $50,000 if you have less than 5 years of experience. Aim too high and you won't get calls. Aim too low and you've sold yourself short.*

<u>Tips for your Resume & Cover Letter:</u>
Don't list your salary range in your cover letter, or list an exceptionally large range, such as a $10,000 spread. On your resume, show progression in your career. If you were promoted at a company, be sure to mention it. Your Work History will need to show growth, whether by moving up in one company or by taking more responsibility. Even better, know the percentage of salary increases when it comes time to negotiate salary. The average person changes jobs for 5-10% more salary. If your pattern has been 10-20% in the past, this is justification for seeking that much now.

Most importantly, make sure there is a reason for the increased salary. Longevity is not enough in a sour economy. More than ever, HR departments are gauging a candidate's worth based on their last salary. It's why they now ask for that information in a screening interview. Anticipate this objection and have a solid case for getting more money.

Samples follow...

Figure 7.11: Cover letter and resume for Increased Salary Expectation

---

INCREASING SALARY CANDIDATE

Address - Phone - Email

Dear Sirs:

Your qualifications for your Marketing Coordinator position listed on craigslist.com seem to be tailor-made to my abilities. Please consider this email as my formal application for your position.

> In my recent position as the Office Manager for XXX company, coordinating complex projects was my specialty. Some of these advanced tasks included coordinating all of our marketing materials and managing all of our social media marketing.

This paragraph highlights relevant experience that they may not recognize

> In addition to my work experience, I just graduated college with my degree in marketing. I look forward to applying these principles into the work environment.

This is the kicker justifying the increase in salary

> Creative problem solving and ownership of my position have always been critical for the success of my employers. Working independently, setting personal deadlines and prioritizing are part of my very nature.

Soft skills or personality traits that support the higher salary

Please feel free to contact me at xxx if you have any questions, however, please keep in mind that my job search is confidential. I would love for an opportunity to discuss putting my varied skills to your advantage.

Sincerely,

Upwardly Mobile Candidate

INCREASING SALARY CANDIDATE

Address - Phone - Email

MARKETING COORDINATOR

Dedicated and a proven hard worker, I bring a unique mix of talents that make a successful marketing professional: creative, enthusiastic, organized and detail-oriented while never losing sight of the big picture. My real-world experience combined with my excellent education make me the ideal marketing coordinator, ready to tackle any challenge with proven problem-solving and project management skills.

EDUCATION

Bachelor of Science in Marketing, *College of Denver*, Denver, CO
Expected Graduation Date: December 2011

Student Club Involvement:
- American Marketing Association (AMA)
- Student Marketing Association (SMA)

Associate of Arts, Liberal Arts College, *Anytown, USA*
Graduated: December 2007

TECHNICAL SKILLS AND NATURAL ABILITIES

- Advanced MS Office
- Intermediate in Microsoft Outlook
- Skilled in Adobe Photoshop, Illustrator
- Database applications

- Interpersonal and communication skills
- Highly organized and detail-oriented
- Self-motivated and determined
- Social media applications

PROFESSIONAL EXPERIENCE

NATIONAL COMPANY, ANYTOWN, USA   **May 2007 - Present**
Office Manager / Marketing Assistant

Personally took control of a chaotic office to create an efficient and effective workspace for the team
- Organized all marketing materials
- Managed the Outlook data base, organizing hundreds of prospective client contacts
- Created and managed all client files, in both hard copy and electronic forms
- Prepared and submitted expense reports for the team
- Coordinated conventions and trade show attendance
- Designed documents from rough directions
- Performed online research and social media marketing
- Initial point of contact for a high volume of customers

<u>NOTES:</u>

Responsibilities beyond your title

Perception Problem: are you being honest? Will not see your full scope of ability; screeners make judgments on titles.

Ways to overcome the Perception:
Be sure to mention all of your duties in your resume. Be prepared to speak about this at length in the interview.

Tips for your Resume & Cover Letter:
There are a few ways to handle the additional duties scenario. First of all, add a Key Achievements section to the beginning of your resume. This helps the additional duties stand out. Next, you can list the additional titles in (parentheses) in your resume (see Figure 7.12). This helps not only with computerized screeners that are looking for the title, it helps humans understand what you mean.

Be clear in your Cover Letter that you were assuming additional responsibilities and why. In recent years, people are taking on more and more varied roles - be sure you get credit for all the extra work you've done.

Samples follow...

Figure 7.12: Cover letter and resume for Duties Beyond Your Title

Duties Beyond the Title Candidate

Executive Personal Assistant
Dedicated ‖ Talented ‖Resilient

Dear Sirs:

I am very interested in the Executive Assistant position listed on craigslist.com.

> ➤ In fact, much of my past eight years experience in the office management, accounting and non-profit work has provided me with skills that you would desire, especially my with my knack for keeping track of details. Furthermore, I thrive on interaction with a wide variety of people, from part-time employees to the CEOs of Fortune 500 Companies across the country.

| Point out the facts of why you are relevant |

> ➤ In my most recent position with Renewable Energy, I moved up from the Office Manager position to being the Staff Accountant. However, I was not a typical accountant; a good deal of my job involved documenting procedures and writing training manuals. Additionally, I managed many of the Executive Assistant functions, including international travel and drafting executive communication.

| Highlight the duties beyond the title |

I enjoy the variety of Personal Assitant work and would welcome an opportunity to use a variety of my skills again.

Please feel free to contact me at 720-341-8229 if you have any questions. I would love for an opportunity to discuss putting my varied skills to your advantage.

Sincerely,

Diligent Applicant

Duties Beyond the Title Candidate

Address ✦ phone ✦ email

Executive Personal Assistant

Dedicated ‖ Talented ‖ Resilient

I am a natural leader, developing teams of service providers by displaying my empathy, honesty, integrity and compassion. In short, I am the Executive Assistant that can handle every nuance of your work with professionalism, competency and grace.

Key Achievements

- Managed office relocation and build-out from 2,500 sf to 7,000 sf office
- Revised Employee Handbook and over 100 Policy & Procedure documents
- Created fund-raising events for over 1,000 guests, raising over $100K for charity
- Proven ability to coordinate extensive schedules across international time zones

Skills Summary

- Office (Word, Excel, PowerPoint, Outlook)
- Professional Correspondence
- Event Coordination and Planning
- International Travel Coordination
- Personable and Confidential
- Detail-oriented and thorough
- Intelligent and adaptable
- Willing to travel

Professional Experience

Office Manager/ Staff Accountant (Acting Executive Assistant) 2007 – Present
Renewable Energy, Anytown, USA

- Develops billing procedures for new products and clients
- Responsible for coordinating a major office relocation, including supervision $180K furniture purchase and acting as point-of-contact for office build-outs
- Managed vendors, including evaluating and recommending the VoIP telephone
- Organization of critical documents using Policy IQ and Adobe Acrobat, including Company Policies & Procedures and Due Diligence documentation
- Coordinated executive travel arrangements

Concierge Service/ Personal Assistant   2004 - 2007
Anytown, USA

For several years, provided assistances to a select group of executives and their families.

- Organized homes, including closets, kitchens, personal finances and home office
- Project research and liaison for selling homes and/or valuable household items
- Extensive personal errands, household shopping and gift shopping/ wrapping
- Event coordination and selection of private chefs

Final words on discrepancies

Nothing in your past is insurmountable. Even people with criminal records can find employers willing to hire them; it just may take longer.

No matter what your situation, you need to think of things from the employer's point of view. If you can speak comfortably and confidently about any issue, your strength as a candidate increases exponentially. The key is your own self-perception.

Chapter 8 - The Hidden Job Market

In the recruiting world, there are two types of candidates: active and passive. Active candidates are conducting job searches, posting their resumes, looking for job openings and applying for positions. Passive candidates are not actually looking for a job, or at least not looking very hard. They may be contacted out of the blue by a headhunter, who is trying to entice them away from their current employer. Passive candidates are chosen for their stability, their special talents or their accomplishments in the industry.

Employers can be active or passive as well. Active employers are posting jobs on public sites, reviewing candidates and conducting interviews. In a passive state, they may not realize their need yet. Here lies the magic of the unadvertised job: pure anticipation of needs.

Use your expertise to anticipate the employer's needs. Not everyone can do this; if you are able to determine a company's needs based on current situations, it is a huge asset. Timing is another critical factor. It is not enough to be aware of the targeted employer. You must be aware of the overall industry changes, trends within your geographical area and other factors in the professional landscape.

To accomplish a successful bid for an unadvertised job, you need to roll up your sleeves and do as much research as possible. It not only lands the job, it makes it easier to be effective from the first day.

Research Tools to Track Down the Hiring Manger
As an active candidate, you need to do more than scan the employment websites. You need to be in constant contact with your industry. Pay attention to the news, read the business papers and check out the trade magazines. Be alert to changes and trends. Which company just landed a major contract? Are new products or technologies being introduced? What are the consumers buying?

Figuring out industry trends gives you a huge advantage. All too many job seekers focus on the posted jobs and forget to look at the bigger picture. Even if you focus your search mostly on advertised jobs, being knowledgeable about current events makes you shine in the interview.

What you need to find

When it comes to researching contacts at a company, many candidates make the mistake of trying to find the contact information for the HR recruiter. That is *never* the target... what you want to find are the hiring managers.

Not sure who the hiring manager is? No problem. You actually want to send your resume and cover letter to any possible manager. This not only covers all of your bases, but also creates a possible networking source. For example, if you send your resume to Bob but Bill is the actual hiring manager, Bob may forward your resume to the right person. That carries more weight than just a blind email.

This can get time-consuming, but it is worth it. When you get your resume directly into the hiring manager's hands, he or she can resurrect you from the cut pile - assuming, of course, that your cover letter and resume are focused.

There is more to this research than just generating names, email addresses and phone numbers. It even goes farther than just reading up on the industry. In fact, you need to find out as much information as possible on any potential hiring manager or company. Diving deep into the resources is what sets an exceptional candidate apart from just being good.

Targeting specific companies

The first order of business is to determine your target companies. Start with 10 and then build from there. If you are pursuing jobs in multiple fields, choose ten companies for each of the industries. It may be necessary to focus all of your efforts on one industry at a time, to avoid confusion.

Not sure about companies in your area? Check out these resources to find lists of companies in your area:

- Better Business Bureau
- Chambers of Commerce in your area
- Local business magazines, such as the Denver Business Journal

- Manta.com - free source that complies information from government sources. Companies can expand on their information for free.
- ResourceUSA.com - data base of multiple sources across the US. All you need is a library card to access it.
- Zoominfo.com - information on large to medium sized companies

Once you find some potential companies, start with their website. Look beyond the employment opportunities or careers pages. Strive to gain a clear picture of this company, from the mission statement to their product line. Look at their press releases. What are they doing to make the news? What are their marketing campaigns? Where do they advertise? Make note of any changes to key personnel, such as managers or executives; it is common for new leaders to bring in new talent.

Go beyond reading their material

Google the company – what is the rest of the world saying about them? What news stories have been picked up? Are customers writing reviews about them? Is the feedback positive or negative? If you notice a strong faction of complaints, this could be a solution you can offer the company. Similarly, you may discover a lot of complaints from previous employees and may determine that this is not a company you want to work for. Research is about eliminating unfavorable employers as well.

Social Media as a research tool

For key personnel, see if you can find their profiles on the business networking site, www.linkedin.com. Think about it like Facebook for business. Of the 100+ million users, it is estimated that more than half are in management. You can search for people by name, company, location and several other criteria. LinkedIn will show you a person's profile, but may not be able to connect to them directly. It depends on the other person's settings, as well as your own account - people with paid accounts can see more information on other people's profiles. If you can't connect, look at what groups your target has joined. Many people list their groups directly on their profile; once you share a group, you can send an email or connection invitation directly to your target - without having to pony up for a paid account. Other people in your network can introduce you as well; LinkedIn will show you which of your connections may know the target.

Not finding the contacts or getting overwhelmed with the results generated in a basic search? Look for the "advanced search" feature right next to the search field. This allows you to narrow your search by location, industry, company name and even if this is a current job or not.

LinkedIn groups are a great way to connect with others or to start building an online reputation. You need to join two kinds of groups: large, local groups and industry-specific groups. For example, the Linked to Denver group has over 16,000 members (as of December 2011). When you join that group, you instantly have a group connection with all of those members. Chances are you won't engage in too many of the discussions on a big group like this, but your strategy is to catch the connections. On the other hand, you do want to be involved in your industry-specific groups. Become an active member: engage in discussions, comment on news or post articles. This way, you can start raising awareness of who you are by participating in intelligent, online discussion - this makes it easier to connect with people online.

Speaking of Facebook, many companies are using this website to create their own business fan pages. With over 500 million users world-wide, it is a cheap and easy way for businesses to reach their target market. By following the company itself, you can compare their official public relations spin versus what an individual manager or employee may say. Not only

Another option is www.twitter.com. If their profile is public, you can follow them to see what they post throughout the day. Even companies are creating Twitter accounts to reach their target markets. Follow them to see what they say about themselves. Is their marketing effective or not? What image are they promoting?

One word of caution with Twitter: be careful what you post yourself. Twitter lets people post things instantly from either their computer or mobile device. These short posts are forwarded to everyone following you, including potential employers. As a fast communication tool, people don't stop and think about what they are posting. Don't rant and rave about your current boss online. Don't gripe about family members or friends. Don't post in times of anger, resentment or depression.

A Great Truth

Social networking may or may not get you a job, but it can certainly cost you one.

Here's another thought: employers are looking at candidate's online profiles more than ever before. Previously, employers would research online personas as part of the background check. Now, when you contact potential employers through Facebook, Twitter or LinkedIn, *they will look at your profile to decide if they will even respond to you.* Be sure that your online profiles are portraying the correct professional image. Don't forget to check your spelling within your emails, invites, LinkedIn conversations and Twitter postings. A few seconds of blazing a post as fast as you can could ruin your chances for a job.

The internet is full of stories where the candidate gets a job offer, only to have it rescinded because of an inappropriate Twitter or Facebook post. My personal favorite was the job candidate who tweeted "I don't really want this job, but I will take their money." Now he has neither the job nor the money. D'oh!

Monitor your target companies' competition

This tactic has two advantages: looking for market trends and uncover another possible employment source. Offering a future employer an edge over their competition - hiring you - is a great pitch to potential hiring managers. Managers want someone who is in touch with the industry. If you watch all the key players, your industry knowledge becomes a true competitive advantage.

Use the government as a source

In addition to the local Work Force Center, the government has a lot of valuable research tools for the public at no cost. Statistical information from the Bureau of Labor Statistics and the US Census give indications of rising industries and professions.

Additionally, you can monitor the various government agencies to find regulatory changes that impact your industry. For example, the Federal Communications Commission (FCC) regulates the broadcast industry. If you are interested in that industry, watch for new laws or regulations coming up.

Sweeping changes take some time to initiate. Being aware of these impending changes can give you a powerful edge, plus enough lead-time to take advantage of them. Think of sitting in an interview with the hiring manager and discussing the newest law affecting your industry. You look like someone who is really in touch with what's going on – and this definitely raises the manager's opinion of you.

Charities and non-profits

Most people contact charities for jobs after the organization has received a big grant or donation. This is a perfectly acceptable use of your research. However, large corporate gifts provide leads as well. Companies who can afford to support non-profits tend to be more stable. Sponsorship gives you a great feel for the corporate culture of your target – what causes do they support? How do they stay connected to the community? What is the benefit to them for the donations: free press, marketing material or connecting their company to a specific value set? Basically, do they do it out of principles or for recognition? Who are they trying to influence?

* * *

How to Use Your Research

Knowledge is a great tool, but you have to know how to use it. When you create your cover letter and resume for your target managers, look to your Key Element Detector™ for the basics and build from there. Now take it to the next level and use your research in your writing, always addressing (you guessed it) the employers' needs – but in this case, you have to address their *future needs*, not just the current situation.

Figure 8.1: Cover letter incorporating recent news

Dr. Henry Jones, CEO
XYZ Company
123 Fake St
Springfield, IL 12345

Dear Mr. Jones:

I have been impressed with XYZ Company's recent expansion in the Midwest. While the opening of your new plant in Chicago is still a few months away, I'm certain that you are already thinking of ways to keep costs down to maximize your profits.

I believe I can help you reach this goal. With my experience as a Plant Manager, I worked with management before the plant was open to make sure we were cost-effective and profitable from the first day. I am excellent at hiring staff to man the production process, choosing critical talent while staying within budgetary guidelines.

I am mindful of OSHA guidelines in creating a safe work environment. By anticipating these standards before the plant was open, we were able to meet legal requirements while choosing the most cost-effective measures.

I would be very interested in discussing your plans for the new plant in detail. I can be reached at 303-555-1212 or through email at plantmanager@yahoo.com.

Sincerely,
John Smith

This is a very effective cover letter for four reasons:

1. It was sent to the right person – in this case, the president of the company.

2.   <u>It is written in the industry's language</u> – referring to meeting OSHA guidelines plus using management's language of money.

3.   <u>It speaks intelligently about the industry</u> – relevant experience is referenced right away.

4.   <u>It addresses the company's future needs</u> in ways they might not have fully thought about yet.

Get to the right person

Have you seen offers to send your cover letter and resume to all the CEOs in your industry? This practice is called "resume blasting." It is not based on research or forethought at all. Instead, the service sends your resume and form cover letter is emailed to a list of CEOs, anywhere from 100 to 1,000, depending on how much you pay. The theory plays upon a numbers game: if you throw enough resumes out there, something will eventually stick.

A Great Truth

Resume blasting never works. Only personalized, insightful and intelligent communication will get the attention of the hiring manager.

Management and their assistants recognize a form letter when they see it, and will treat it like any other piece of spam. They toss it in the trash.

Only personalized cover letters are effective. If you aren't writing to a specific person and his situation, you are wasting your time and theirs. You need the manager's name, title and area of influence. Contact information is vital, especially the email address.

Check the employer's website first. Many companies list their top executives by name, and some will even list their contact information. If not, try LinkedIn again - search the company's name and add any title with "executive" or "president" in the advance search features. This will reveal Vice Presidents, Executives and Executive Assistants. Assistants can be a great back door to the management team. If you can get their attention, they may forward your information to the manager. Plus, you can ask for their preferred method of communication: email, mail or phone call. Assistants are valuable when trying to determine the direction of a company as well. Hunting for the managers or team leads? Try the same tactic, especially since employees at this level may not be on the company's website.

If these tactics don't work, you can still get that contact information.

Call the main phone number, but don't ask for your target person right away. Instead, mention that you are updating your mailing list *or* that so-n-so gave you an email address and you want to confirm the information. Follow the pattern of other email addresses on their website to guess the format (bill.jones@xyzcompany.com, for example). Even if the receptionists or assistant asks you to send them the information first, take that. Now you have the company's format for email addresses. (Don't send your resume to the receptionist, by the way. This was only a test to get the email format.)

If all else fails with an electronic submission, mail a hard copy. The company's mailing address is easy to find. If you do mail your materials, you must use good resume stock paper, with matching envelope. Include your business card if you have one. On the envelope, type the addresses. When you mail them a hard copy, everything will be scrutinized, especially for an unadvertised job. Your presentation should support the fact that you are a powerhouse candidate.

* * *

Networking – Does It Really Work?

Is networking valuable? Like everything else, it depends on how you use it. If you're just calling people and asking for jobs, then no, it does not. If you can offer something of value – knowledge, experience or even friendship – then yes, it can.

The 80% myth: "80% of all job seekers find jobs by networking."
Heard that one yet? Scary, isn't it? Many candidates are not comfortable with networking. Not everyone is as personable or bold

as the super-salesman, after all. Believe it or not, shy and introverted people get hired every day.

The 80% figure is an inflated number. It includes Aunt Martha telling you about a job she saw on Monster.com. You don't have to shake hands like a politician to land a job. Don't get intimidated or down on yourself if this is a weak area for you. There are plenty of ways to improve your networking skills.

Get over networking fear

If you're not comfortable with face-to-face networking, try it online first. Websites like www.linkedin.com and www.facebook.com are great places to contact people. If you can break the ice in electronic worlds, you will be more confident when you meet people face-to-face. Social networking sites are growing exponentially, which opens more and more back doors to your target companies. However, there is more to gain than just job contacts. Networking is really about people helping each other by sharing knowledge. This is done in groups.

When you join groups, ask questions and get involved. If you like someone's answers, look at his profile. Is this somebody you would like to know more about? Try emailing them in private about their answers, rather than just posting your comments in the discussion areas. After you've shared some emails back and forth, ask them to connect. They don't have to work for your immediate target companies to be valuable. The goal is to build a self-sustaining network that will last beyond the job search.

Learn to build a *valuable network*. It's not really about building the numbers if you have no idea who these people are or what your connection to them is. As in real life, concentrate on building mutually beneficial business relationships. In my own case, I have found mentors, students, advisors, old acquaintances, friends and fun people online. Isn't that what true networking is all about?

Once you get accustomed to reaching out to people, *then* go after your targets, seeking them on LinkedIn and Twitter. Just like anything, networking is a skill and you become better by practicing it. If you've started to build your network already, you will quickly become a valued asset instead of "that creepy guy" who tracks people down and bombards them with silly or irrelevant emails.

Going live: Professional groups and associations
Professional associations are valuable connections with your industry. Use these as research centers and build up from there.

In general, many professional groups contain a significant number of job seekers, about 10-30% of their membership. Don't go to a meeting thinking you're going to meet the CEO and hand him your resume. Nobody likes being blindsided at a social function.

Instead, ask them questions about their company and industry. The more you can ask about *them*, the better. People like to talk about themselves. Ask intelligent questions – you might even write some down before you get to the event to help keep your own focus:

- Where do you see your company going in the future?

- I read an article about _____ - what's your opinion?

- I think _____ is going to be a big industry trend – what do you think?

- What's your biggest challenge right now?

The last question is a great lead-in. If you get an opportunity to pitch yourself, be sure it relates to the needs they just stated.

When you meet people at a networking event, be sure to trade business cards. If you don't have any, www.VistaPrint.com has some very affordable options for cards that look and feel professional. Keep your message positive, and not a desperate title like "Seeking opportunities in Human Resources."

After the event, it is essential to follow up the next day. Send a thank you email and mention key points you discussed the day before, even if it was fantasy football or the latest movies. You want your new contact to remember you – many people don't recall names, but will remember an interesting conversation.

Don't send your new contact a resume right away. Cultivate the relationship first. Show appreciation for them as a person, not just an avenue to get a job. Networking works best when you *connect* with people, not *use them*.

Networking groups

Over the past years, networking groups have become more prominent. Unlike professional associations, networking groups can be comprised of other job seekers. Some groups offer support, others provide a presentation of some facet of job searching. Another type is like a "speed networking" format: each person gets to share for about two minutes, stating who they are, what they are looking for and some of their target companies. Then other group members offer them names of contacts within those companies.

You can find a number of live, in-person networking groups through the social media site www.Meetup.com. In fact, you can find groups there for any interest or passion, from Star Wars fans to single mingles. Joining some groups that are not related to job searching brings another level of contacts - plus, it gets you out of the house and involved in something you enjoy. Most groups are free or minimal cost, so it is a great way to find affordable entertainment options.

* * *

Aggressive Techniques

If you are comfortable with approaching people, you can try aggressive approaches. These are high-pressure techniques and they don't work for every industry, or even every job. To pull this off, you really have to sell yourself – making these tactics ideal for salesmen, marketing people or anyone seeking a results-driven job.

Informational interview

When you set up an informational interview, you will be interviewing someone inside the company to gain more insight into their structure, mission or industry. This technique is frequently used by college graduates or people making a career transitions, but anyone can do it. Often times, you want to set up an informational interview for a contact from a networking group.

Some companies are open to formal tours. Check with the public relations or promotions department to explore this option. During your tour of the facility, use prepared questions to find out more about the company. This can be anything from their manufacturing process to how many employees work there. On a formal tour, you may not meet anyone of significance, but it is all knowledge you can use in your job search.

For an informational interview, try to arrange an interview with one of your target managers, his assistant or someone in his department. Don't bother with human resources; chances are, they won't have time for a 10-minute conversation about the company.

When you call, be clear about your motives, which is to find out more about the company. It is NOT asking for a job! Your focus? Find out as much about the company you possibly can. Prepare your questions ahead of time. If your research brought up questions, be sure to address those. You must be concise with these phone interviews, as you will only get 10-15 minutes.

Whether you meet people in person or on the phone, ask intelligent questions. If you can prove that you are bright, knowledgeable and excited about their company, you can gain an introduction to the right people. I have seen people who conducted informational interviews that didn't result in a job offer, but their interviewee did pass on their resume to other contacts who were hiring.

15 minute presentation

Contact the CEO or Manager directly. Follow this up with phone calls. Your goal is to get a 15-minute appointment to give a presentation. This is *not* an interview, and don't call it that at any point. Your presentation is either a cost-saving suggestion or a way to increase revenue. What's the product? It's you, of course.

After the presentation, offer samples of your work. This could be presented as an "audition", where you work at a greatly reduced rate for a limited period of time. During this trial period, you need to make an impact right away to prove everything you just promised.

* * *

Final words on research

You don't have to be a super-aggressive extrovert to find an unadvertised job. The keys are research, good timing and a belief in your own abilities.

Use both online and in-person networking techniques to build contacts in your industry. Your goal should not be landing the job, but creating a network that will retain its value beyond this job search. True networking means forming real relationships, sharing knowledge and gaining strength from each other. If you're only pursuing contacts to get a job, your network will be hollow and not self-sustaining.

If you can accurately anticipate an organization's needs, you are golden. Keep all of your materials and communications focused on answering their needs.

Chapter 9 - Finding a Job Online

Electronic job searching has become the staple for many job seekers. It's easy, it's fast and it can be done at home. Unfortunately, it's also easy and fast to do it very poorly. This is why you have probably heard the horrible rumors about it: "nobody finds a job on those websites – it's just a resume black hole."

That's not true, by the way. It is possible to navigate the HR procedures and land a job you found on Monster, CareerBuilder or any of the other online sources. It just takes some effort and solid job searching tools.

What is electronic job searching?
Electronic job searching includes any online job lead. This includes the traditional sites such as Monster.com, CareerBuilder and even Craigslist. However, electronic job searching also includes social media, networking groups, company websites and personal websites. You are only limited by your imagination and how much work you put into it.

Print is dead
Don't waste your time looking through the printed newspaper – newspapers place all of those ads on their websites free-of-charge to the employers. In fact, many employers won't waste resources printing their ads anymore. A print ad for one Sunday costs an employer from $400 to $800; an internet ad will stay active for 30 days and only cost them about $300.

Most local newspapers link their job posting with a major online resource, such as Jobing.com. However, local papers can be good leads for lower-level jobs, high demand fields (such as nursing) or a local niche. Look at your local paper's website to gauge for yourself how valuable this source might be. Just one Sunday edition will be enough to determine if it is worth your time.

Effective use of employment websites
The first step for online job searching is to put all your tools in place, ready to use. Establish an account with the major employment sites,

upload your resume and create your job search agent (don't worry, I'll explain all that). Take the time to do this first. Then you can maximize the time you spend online researching applying for jobs. Once you invest the initial set-up time, you can find and apply for jobs within a few hours each week. This gives you time for more advanced research and networking.

Tips for setting up your account:

1. Write your resume off-line

Don't use the "build your resume" functions of the website. This encourages poor writing and grammatical or spelling errors.

2. Upload different resume versions

Most websites allow you to upload up to five different resumes. When you apply to a job, you choose which resume to send. This is especially helpful if you are looking for jobs in multiple disciplines.

3. Draft some stock cover letters

You can always customize any cover letter when you apply, but having some good, stock cover letters ready can help save time.

4. Determine your targets and terminology

Think about different ways your target jobs might be listed. Define the jobs by title, function, career-level, location and key words. Sometimes what you think is the right term may not be used in the industry at all. Experiment with different searches on each website to figure out what works best for your desired results.

Safety Tips For Your Job Search

One of my Denver clients recently called me with an unfortunate but common problem:

> *"I just got called by the police – they discovered an identity theft ring which had stolen my information from an online job application," he said, totally despondent and heartbroken. "I guess I'm lucky because the cops caught them, but I still have to deal with cleaning up the mess they made…"*

In recent years, identity theft and other scams that target job seekers has seen a sharp increase. It is estimated that 50% of job ads on craigslist.com are fraudulent. Compared to a rate of approximately 30% in 2008, it is easy to see that the thieves are banking on the desperation of the job seekers.

Fortunately, you can easily protect yourself from such scams.

Protect your information
One of the common tricks is to direct job seekers to an online application. While many legitimate companies use online applications, or Applicant Tracking Systems (ATS), look out for ones that require too much personal information.

If the application asks for any of this information, do NOT fill it in:
- Social Security number
- Birth Date (they should only ask if you are over 18)
- Bank account information (often disguised as trying to set up your direct deposit)
- Mother's maiden name (often needed to establish credit)
- Previous names used
- Insistence on full salary history when you apply

If you are still interested in the job after running into these requests, call the company first. If their name is not listed on the website, definitely run the other way.

Private resume posting
Scammers are also contacting people who place their resumes online. Generally speaking, do NOT post your resume online unless you can do so in a completely private manner.

In cases like Craigslist that offers no privacy settings on resume posting, do not post your resume at all.

Don't accept packages
A newer twist from scammers is the offer to help someone run their purchasing business. Usually coming from someone across the country or who "travels a lot," the job sounds like a great way to make

part time money. All you have to do is receive the packages and ship them forward.

The first few deals may work out. However, then as you "prove yourself" on the job, you get asked to make purchases on the employer's behalf, with a promise to pay you back plus interest. Here the scam can run two ways: either you never get reimbursed, or else the employer asks for your banking information to send you money.

Anytime someone asks for banking info is a bad sign…

Legitimate professional shoppers or art dealers do not operate this way. They already have a network that they use for these services.

Work at home
While there are many legitimate work-at-home opportunities, you do need to be careful. Here are some of the common work-at-home scams:

- You have to pay for training
- You have to buy materials to assemble items for resale (either you can't sell the items, or the "employer" won't pay you for the work performed
- Stuffing envelopes – there are machines that do this 10,000 times faster than you; why would they pay?
- Bogus direct deposit forms

If you are serious about a work-from-home opportunity, check out www.Flexjobs.com. While you do have to pay to see the full jobs listings, Flexjobs researches each and every job to make sure they are a legitimate offering from a real company.

Check local resources
Before you apply for any job, you should research the company. In particular, resources like Colorado's Better Business Bureau, local Chambers of Commerce (including the internet Chambers of Commerce) and local news sources like the Denver Business Journal all carry information on local businesses. In the case of the Better Business Bureau, they have free information on most of the businesses, whether they are members or not. Seeing the number of complaints – or a lack of records – are all indications that a potential employer is not on the level.

162

Use common sense

While the job search may be driving you crazy, don't let desperation override your common sense. If a deal sounds too good to be true, it probably is.

Evaluate the websites carefully. Do they have postings for your target job? How many? Are they current, say, within the past few weeks? What is the quality of the employers? Most websites will have a large amount of jobs posted by employment agencies, and that's to be expected. Don't completely ignore a website because of the agency volume.

Ads to avoid

MANAGEMENT TRAINING – NO EXPERIENCE NECESSARY!
OFFICE MANAGER – FUN WORKING ENVIRONMENT
INSIDE SALES – TRAINING PROVIDED

Be aware of ads that use capitals, bolding and other attention-grabbing tricks. These jobs might not be scams, but they are less-than-desirable positions. Traditional jobs don't need to shout to gain applicants.

Confidential job postings will not list the name of the employer. That does not mean it's a scam. Employers use this tactic for a variety of reasons. They may be replacing a current employee, or they want to discourage phone calls. If a job grabs your interest, pursue it. Unfortunately, you won't be able to send a personalized cover letter to the hiring manager through a blind ad.

Brand-new websites can be valuable, even if they don't boast a vast number of jobs. The HR department will watch any new recruiting source carefully. Any candidate coming from a new source is considered carefully because the company is judging the quality of the website's candidates. Your chance to make an impact increases because of their scrutiny.

* * *

Where Are The Jobs?

Yes, real people are finding real jobs on the commercial employment sites. This is why you need to include these websites in your job search. However, not all websites are going to serve your needs. Make effective use of your time and concentrate on the avenues that offer the greatest chance of landing your target job.

Different employment sites attract different kinds of employers. Where are your targets advertising? Companies will use whatever source that draws them the most viable and desirable candidates. In some cases, this may be the large sites. In others, an industry-specific site might serve their needs best. Just like in every part of the job search, think in terms of what the employer needs.

Following is a description of several employment websites. *Note:* this is *not* a comprehensive list of all employment websites. Nor is this an endorsement for any or all of these websites. This information is meant to provide a starting point for your job search – if you find another great website that is not part of this list, use it!

Monster.com

As one of the first national employment websites, Monster is well known and many employers post their jobs here. Monster offers free tools for candidates, such as career-specific newsletters, salary comparison links and saved searches. You can load up to five resumes and cover letters on Monster.

CareerBuilder.com

Careerbuilder.com is another major employment website. They frequently have several job postings, mainly because of the competitive pricing to employers. While CareerBuilder lets you upload a Word-version of your resume, it will convert it to text. When you preview the resume, CareerBuilder will show you almost exactly what the employer will receive. CareerBuilder features many free helpful tools, such as categorized searches, public profiles, career advice, newsletters and salary comparisons.

Craigslist.com

Craigslist.com started as a free classified service in several major cities, offering such diverse posting categories as garage sales to personals. Some of the major markets charge for job postings, but the

164

cost is a fraction of the dedicated employment sites. As a result, many small to mid-sized businesses will post the job on craigslist.com first. Even large businesses are catching this idea, especially for administrative support or junior positions. However, because the postings are so cheap, there are more scams. Visit an employers' website before you apply, and never send your salary history. Be very careful about posting your resume on the site itself, as this is a public posting and you cannot control who sees it.

Indeed.com

Indeed.com is a different kind of employment site. Rather than being a single source for jobs, it will search all of the other employment sites for their job postings and then give you the results. This can be a great tool to monitor multiple sites, including government and specific employers' websites. You can even find out about niche industry sites that you might not know about.

LinkedIn.com

Did you know that Linkedin.com has an employment section as well? When you apply, the employers will get your resume *and* your online profile at the same time. Some employers request a certain number of recommendations on your profile before they will consider your resumes, so it is helpful to build your profile fully before going after these jobs.

There is another, secret place where jobs are posted on LinkedIn: in the groups. For most groups, there is a tabbed section called "jobs." The first ones listed under "Jobs" are the paid advertisements that have been reposted in the group. But if you look at the "Job Discussions," you will find a nice surprise.

These jobs have been posted directly by the recruiters - for free. You not only get to the actual job description and how to apply, you see the LinkedIn profile of the recruiter as well. Don't post your resume as a reply. After all, you don't want to clue your competition. Instead, follow the instructions in the job description to apply for the job. And while you're at it, send a nice, personal email or Inmail to the recruiter through LinkedIn to let him or her know of your interest.

TheLadders.com

TheLadders.com is for candidates seeking jobs with an annual salary of $100,000 or more. They could be considered a "pay to play" website; that means you have to pay a monthly fee to apply for jobs, or even to see the full job descriptions. Their monthly fee is actually part of their well-advertised candidate screening service to employers – if you can't afford the monthly fee, you probably aren't serious about a job at this level.

FlexJobs.com

A listing of real part-time, contract and work-from-home opportunities. The company verifies the jobs before listing them. However, you do have to pay a fee to use the site.

Specialty sites

Specialty sites cater to one particular industry, such as Dice.com for Information Technology jobs and EstateJobs.com for private service and luxury domestic staff positions. Other sites may reach out to different parts of society, such as Diversity.com for companies who want to increase diversity in their workforce. If you aren't sure about all of the specialty sites that relate to your industry, use indeed.com to reveal them.

Company websites

Be sure to monitor your top targets on a regular basis. Some companies test a position on their website first to gauge interest. Another tactic is to post one or two jobs on a big site like careerbuilder.com with the hope that it will drive candidates to their website, thereby increasing traffic for minimal cost. Check your top desired companies regularly.

A few others of note

As mentioned before, <u>this is not a comprehensive list</u> of every employment website, but merely ideas to get you going:

- Hard2hire.com – This site features employers willing to work with unusual situations, such as a criminal record, disabilities or older workers.

- Snagajob.com – Hourly, full time and part time jobs

- Usajobs.gov – Government employment opportunities

- Simplyhired.com – Similar to indeed.com search engine, pulling ads from multiple sites

- Talentzoo.com – Advertising, media and marketing jobs

- Salesjobs.com – Sales positions

- Jobing.com – local jobs in various markets, such as Denver and Phoenix. *Note:* many states do have employment sites for local positions only, and it may not be through your local newspaper. Google around to find your local outlet.

An advantage with smaller or newer websites
Employers are always looking for ways to do things better, cheaper and faster. In some cases, this means experimenting with new employment websites. Anytime you apply for a job through a smaller websites, you will get more serious consideration from the employer. Why? They are reading all of the candidates from the new website carefully, to see the quality of candidates the posting generates. Plus, because smaller websites generate less traffic, you will have less competition.

Should you post your resume on the web?
Have you seen the ads giving statistic like "job seekers are more likely to find a job when they post their resume on such-n-such site?" That is true – but it does not mean that your resume has to be visible to the entire world! Be conscious of the different posting options to control your online image.

Public
A public posting allows potential employers to view your resume, even when you did not apply for a job. Your resume and all of your contact information will be visible in a search.

Confidential

A confidential posting is still public, but the website will hide your name and contact information, including the names and place of past or current employers. Recruiters will be able to contact you by email, run through the employment website.

Private

No one can see your resume unless you apply for their job. It will not turn up in general searches. When you apply, the employer does get all of your contact information.

Most people choose to post private – but it is still a posted resume, and that counts towards the job site's sales statistics. Websites use these statistics to sell their services to the employers.

Why would you post it public?

If you choose to post publicly, aggressive recruiters, straight-commission sales jobs or less-than-desirable employers might contact you. However, if you are in a high-demand, high-volume industry such as health care, it might be worth the risk.

When an employer searches through the resume database, it is called *data mining*. Employers pay money - and a lot of it - to conduct a search like this. That's why most employers do not use this feature to find employees. Typically, data mining is used to fill high-turnover positions, such as 100% commission sales jobs. Or worse: it could be a the thinly veiled selling opportunities, such as a "chance" to be your own boss selling insurance – but first you have to pay for your classes, your license, their motivational books, and so on… you get the idea.

If you are not in a high-volume field, post your resume privately. Maintaining control on your online information is an important part of your job search.

A word of caution

If you are considering posting your resume on a 100% public website, such as craigslist.com, think about it very carefully. This opens you to serious risks that go far beyond your job search. It makes your information accessible to scam artists, spammers and any number of unsavory creatures. Reputable employers rarely look at these amateur resume postings. It is recommended that you only post your resume on websites that allow you control over who can and cannot view your information. If you still want to consider posting your resume online in such a forum, read their Personal Safety Tips before you do.

Exception to the rule: Your own private website

Some job seekers need to have a website to display their work, such as artists, marketing, production and other jobs. A private website can give you a platform to load up all kinds of interesting information, including a blog, recommendations and samples of their work.

Many people link their non-traditional online resume with their LinkedIn profile to add to their abbreviated online profile. As job searching continues to evolve, look for new and different ways to get your materials into your targets' hands.

* * *

The Smart Way To Post Your Resume On Employment Websites

With all of the major employment websites, you can choose between two options to post your resume online. You can either upload the Word document or you can go through a step-by-step process to create your resume. In most cases, you want to upload the Word version; however, pay attention to some formatting quirks.

Sometimes you don't have a choice, and you will be forced to use the online forms. This is often the case with online applications for a particular company. In that case, you do have to cut-and-paste various parts of your resume into their forms. Since you have already created your Word resume in a modular format, each portion should stand on its own. Never try to type a brand-new resume in these forms; filling out forms creates bad writing. Even worse, you won't have spell-check or grammar indicators.

Always review any resume – whether you build it online or written in Word – before hitting the "submit" button. A few moments of review can make a difference between surviving the screening or turning into HR road kill.

How does your word resume look online?

Regardless of how you post your resume, there is a good chance that your formatting will be stripped, without warning and without your knowledge.

Some internet sites are deceptive about this issue. When you navigate to the "employer view," it looks just like your Word document. However, this is not what the employer will see.

A Great Truth

About 50% of the time, employers will receive a text version of your resume - regardless of what the website allows you to preview. This is why you want to avoid the text conversion issues and send a Word or PDF version of your resume directly to the hiring manager.

Many employment websites send employers the text version of your resume. When you apply for a job, the HR department receives an email containing the text resumes – and yes, it is in the body of the email, not an attachment. Within the email is a link to the posted Word version; perhaps the HR department will be impressed enough to click the link. However, this violates the Third Rule for Dealing with HR: Don't Create Extra Work. Multiply this step by 500+ applicants and it's easy to see why they use your text resume rather than track down the Word document.

Once the format is lost, only your words remain to make an impact.

Computer assumptions

Both commercial employment sites and individual employers will transfer your Word resume information into their own forms for their database or Applicant Tracking System (ATS). The forms are their backbone for the system. The system will catalogue and evaluate you, according to the information on your resume or in the stand-alone fields.

In any sizable company, these systems are indispensible for managing the flood of applications. As a job seeker, you will have to accept them as a necessary evil. Even when you've sent your resume to the hiring manager, you still need to apply through the company's online application. You don't want to be discredited because you didn't follow instructions outlined in the job posting. Since the system is critical to your job hunt, don't fall victim to bad assumptions on the computer's part.

The computer will assume your critical information based on common resume formats. This could be your job titles, company names, employment dates and education levels. While you can minimize some of the assumptions by keeping your critical information easily accessible, you still need to check the computer's work.

After you post your resume, take the time to review the summary pages or the applicant information fields. Verify that the information is correct. Look for missing pieces; sometimes if the computer doesn't recognize a section, it overlooks it. This is particularly hazardous for references, summaries and skill sets.

For your skill set, you may need to re-enter each and every skill along with proficiency levels. It can be very time-consuming, but keep in mind that HR will use this information in screening and in making recommendations.

One issue with any online application or posted resume is that cover letters are an after-thought, as are references. Make sure to include yours because they can be a screening tool that some employers use to cut people. It is acceptable to paste a cover letter in the body of your resume to ensure it is included in the ATS. Add your references to the end of your Word resume as well.

A Note on education

Always list your degree, even if it is in an unrelated field. Education is a common screening tool, and the fact that you have a degree at all can make a difference. However, this does not mean that a lack of a degree will automatically screen you out. Many hiring managers don't care about the degree, so long as you can perform the work. Other careers demand a specific degree. How can you tell the difference?

Refer to your Key Element Detector again – how important is the degree? Is a general degree, such as "BA/BS preferred," or do you need a specific one, such as "BA in Human Resources required?" The more detailed the request, the more important the degree is.
?

A Great Truth

A formal college degree can help your chances, but it is not a requirement for success in all industries or positions. Only your Key Element Detector™ can show if a degree is an absolute necessity for your target job.

When you double-check the computerized entries, take note of how much information you can include in the fields. You may have a chance to pull out more information on the forms than what is listed on your resume. For example, the forms might allow you to enter your major and minor, or areas of special study. Unfortunately, the opposite may be true as well. Some of your resume's critical details could be sacrificed because the ATS lacks fields beyond the degree, year and school. If that's the case, you might need to re-emphasize this aspect of your background in your cover letter, especially if you are a new college graduate or if the degree is critical for your job.

Commercial employment websites like Monster emphasize degrees. This makes sense since many of their advertisers are colleges. They promote the importance of actual college experience. Don't be shaken if their advertising or marketing tactics make your feel less secure about your own education. Your Key Element Detector™ will do more to focus your educational needs than any advertisement.

Look for ways to include non-formal education, such as workshops or classes that are listed as "professional development" on your resume. Computerized systems often fail to pull this information from a resume.

Dating yourself

You may be an older job seeker and you left your graduation date off your resume to mask the fact. Unfortunately, the system may force you to re-enter it. Some ATS require complete information or they won't let you continue to the next screen. It might also look strange to you if your work experience is limited to 15 years, but you graduated

25 years ago. It can be tempting to fill in the extra dates to show consistent employment.

If you choose to add any of this information, remember that the hiring manager won't see these details. What he cares about is the fact that you have a degree, relevant experience and the right skills. HR will give him the summary of the other information. To survive the screening, enter your complete information and reduce your risks.

Multiple resumes

Most sites allow you to post more than one resume, although only one can be public at a time. Title your resumes to indicate focus. Keep in mind that your resume title will be visible to employers, so choose something descriptive, such as "Detail Oriented Executive Assistant" or "Motivated Sales Professional." With each resume that you upload, you will need to go back and correct the computer assumptions again.

Special offers and upgrades on resume posting

Throughout the process of posting your resume, you will get a lot of advertising. Don't get cynical - this is how websites pay for their free services to you. That doesn't mean you have to buy anything, including offers from the website itself. Think about what they are really offering; what sounds like a desirable service may not deliver the punch you're expecting. Here are a few examples:

Preferred Viewing or Resume Upgrade

A preferred viewing moves your resume to the top of the list during a recruiter's search. What they aren't telling you is that the preferred view applies to data mining. Remember the recruiters with the high-turnover jobs? If you pay for this service, you just became #1 on their list. Preferred viewing adds no value to the jobs you apply for directly, because they have no influence on an employer's independent ATS or databases. The ATS or the HR person will rate you based on your relevant qualifications, not your paid delivery service.

Resume Blasting

Resume blasting takes your pre-written resume and sends it out to a set list of recruiters or managers. How many

173

depends on the level of service you buy. It seems like you can direct this to your target market because the service does ask for your key words, careers and locations. However, in practice, what they email is a stock cover letter (either yours or one they write for you) and one of your standard resumes. This turns your resume into spam!

Recruiters and managers recognize spam for what it is. If they bother to read it at all, it won't be effective. Why? Because it's a form letter. Employers only respond to cover letters that show your interest in their company. If you send an unsolicited resume, you must knock them dead with your knowledge, special skills and experience. It is not possible to hit a pinpoint target by slinging "stuff" across the employment landscape and hoping something sticks. That is exactly what resume blasting does.

Newsletters and other offers
Personally, I find the newsletters helpful. It keeps my mind focused on my job search, and they generally have good information. However, take all advice with a grain of salt. Some of the techniques can be old and aren't relevant anymore. There might be a gap between marketing theory and what real-world HR people and hiring managers like. Others can be trendy, focusing on techniques that not all employers will understand or use.

For example, some employment newsletters featured articles about unusual interview questions, providing insight into why they are used and how to answer them. In the real world, it is highly unlikely that you will be asked "how many quarters does it take to reach the height of the Empire State Building." These strange questions supposedly gave insight into how you think. Making you sweat was an added bonus. In practice, most interviewers found this technique to be awkward - for them as well as the interviewee.

When reading these newsletters, weigh their advice against your own common sense. Does it sound far-fetched? Is it practical? Is it something that you would be comfortable doing in your own job search? Not all solutions work for all people.

Keep an open mind, but don't let your brains fall on the floor. Sign up for their free newsletters. Stay in touch with the employment game, but don't become discouraged if none of their suggestions seem reasonable to you. You can always cancel the free subscription later.

* * *

Job Search Agents

One of the best tools on established websites are the search agents. Agents allow you to search for your desired position, without having to re-enter all the criteria. You can change your search agents' parameters at any time, and most sites allow for multiple agents. With one click, you can view all the current jobs that match your criteria – but always make note of the date on the job posting. If it's over two weeks old, contact the company to see if the job is still open.

A Great Truth

Your search agent will only be as effective as your criteria. Cast a search that is too narrow and your results will be limited. Make it too broad and you get overwhelmed. Find the balance to empower your job search.

To set up your search agent, base it on an advanced search, not just the standard categories. Using something like "Nursing in Colorado" without further clarification is too broad of a net. Searches start with the general categories, such as location, industry, and experience level. Look for ways to add your own key terms. You will want to keep some variables open. For example, you could choose to exclude all jobs that do not list the salary range, but you probably shouldn't. Less than half employers list the salary in the job ad anymore, and you could miss a job posting because your criteria was too strict. Same thing with failing to consider contract work. You may miss a great opportunity that you didn't consider before.

Consider the employment landscape: if the market is tight, keep the search wider to see various relevant positions. If your specific target is narrow, you will always have fewer results. Decide which tactic serves your needs best.

Agents can email you notifications of new job postings that match your search. This does not mean that your resume was submitted. You still need to go to the website and proactively apply for the job.

* * *

Government and government-sponsored job banks
Government has its own quirks for candidates. Basically, you are required to tell them anything and everything you've ever done. This book does not cover in detail the specific tactics for landing a government job. It requires a different etiquette, tactics and time frame. If you want to work for the government, look at the requirements for application on their website first: www.usajobs.gov. If you are intrigued with the possibilities, invest in some books or classes specifically addressing government positions before you apply.

For finding corporate positions, your local Work Force Center can be another resource. Unemployment requires people to sign up for these Centers. As a source for jobs, it's not the best. Employers send their open job descriptions to the county, and job seekers can search the job bank. However, employers are not required to post their jobs at the Work Force Center, so you still need to check all of the employment websites.

You can use the Work Force Center for training and gaining relevant job skills. They provide testing so you can gauge your abilities or aptitudes. You can explore different career options and discover the requirements. Several Work Force centers host job searching workshops as well. At the bare minimum, you meet the requirements for unemployment benefits.

* * *

Keep track of your resumes
Manage your online information. You may need to update your resume frequently in the early days of your job search. It is easy to lose track of all the resumes you need to update. If you revise one, you have to remember to revise them all – they won't change automatically.

176

Final words on electronic job searching

Online job searching is a critical part of your job search strategy. Take the time to make sure your resume is loaded correctly and that your profile fits with your targets. Be sure to hit the major employment sites, but don't dismiss the newer or smaller websites. Employers will pay more attention to candidates from new sources as they evaluate the website's effectiveness. Keep track of your online information and remember to update all of your accounts at the same time.

Figure 9.1: Resume log

Commercial Employment Sites:

Website	Password	Resume Title(s)	Date Updated	Active Job Search Agents	Loaded Cover Letters	Notes

Target Companies:

Name	Website	Password for ATS	Contact Person	Phone Number	Email Address	Resume Title	Date Applied	Notes

Social Networking Sites:

Website	Password	Profile Focus	Date Updated	Groups	Beneficial Contacts	My Area of Expertise	Questions posed/Answered	Notes

Chapter 10 – 7 Tools HR Uses to Cut You

It's true: HR controls quite a bit of your fate.

In fact, one of the recruiter's biggest functions is to reduce the candidate field for each and every posted job.

A Great Truth

Every single HR department will use simple tricks to screen out the majority of the candidates. Unfortunately, this often includes qualified applicants who didn't understand the hiring process.

HR departments rely on several universal tricks to weed out the candidate pool. Once you are conscious of these tricks, they are easy to overcome. These tricks may seem vicious or insensitive, but HR departments must get rid of 90 - 95% (or more) of the candidates before sending recommendations to the hiring managers. If a job ad pulls in 300 - 500 applicants, only 5 to 10 of them will get an interview. As a result, strict and heartless screening is necessary to get through the onslaught of applicants.

Screening starts before you apply

One of the first problems with the process starts with the job description itself. This document will become the basis of the screening and scoring material, but many of them do not reflect the real needs of the job.

How does that happen?

Ideally, the hiring manager works closely with the HR department to create the job description, devoting time to pinpoint their ideal candidate. In practice, most job descriptions are thrown together haphazardly. The hiring manager is too busy to consult with HR. The HR department adds pieces to fit their format, regardless of the hiring manager's priority. It is a flawed system, sometimes creating a tug-of-war between managers and HR.

A Great Truth

Do hiring managers a favor. Send your cover letter and resume directly to them. Managers can be just as frustrated with the HR process as you are.

Some job descriptions are merely resurrections of an old description and may not reflect current needs. Some job descriptions are very vague and it is hard to guess what the employer wants. For example, sales jobs are notorious for lacking detail - or using such high concept terms that it is difficult to create screening material. Other job descriptions seem like a wish list, asking for an impossibly huge skill set. In that case, the company is "feeling out" a talent pool. They may have many needs, and depending on the applicants, they will alter the actual job to match their top candidate.

Job descriptions are created in three ways:

1. The old job description is resurrected
The hiring manager may read over it to approve it, or she may not. Either way, it is doubtful that this description reflects current needs.

2. The hiring manager starts a frame work
The manager may have a general idea of what he wants, and then gives a draft to the HR department. From there, the HR department puts it in "their format." Often times, they add unnecessary criteria, such as an education level requirement. HR puts it in because that's their policy; it may not be the hiring manager's choice.

3. The hiring manager gives a wish list
Opposite of the skimpy description, a manager may list every single aspect he would want covered. These are often long descriptions, with a seemingly impossible mix of skills. HR won't tell him to make it smaller; their goal is to get the ad placed and start drawing candidates as soon as possible.

This is why your Key Element Detector™ must use several job descriptions to overcome these variables. Only a large sample can weed out the vague and overly detailed to identify the universal aspects of your target job.

Beware of purple squirrels

What the heck is a purple squirrel?

Thanks to the Recession, a new creature has been forged: the purple squirrel. The term was coined by HR departments to describe someone who has skills and experience in a wide variety of areas, such as the Executive Assistant who also does the IT and marketing for the company.

The purple squirrels were created by companies cutting back their staff during the economic downturn. Rather than hire more people or contractors, they began to lean on their remaining staff to "pick up the slack" and help in other areas. Hence why the administrative assistant is now in charge of maintaining the website...

The problem arises when the purple squirrel leaves. Now the employer is looking for someone with that weird skill set mix. They really don't want to hire two people; they want a candidate who can do it all. Unfortunately, this is really hard to do. The odd job mix was based on their specific situation. So what are the options?

Two things happen: they either hire one person who has the essential core skills and train them in the supplemental job functions; or they hire a lower-level employee and train an existing employee to pick up the other area of responsibility.

If you see a job description pop up that asks for a bizarre mix of experience or skills, just keep in mind that they are hunting for a purple squirrel... and by the way, most of these critters left that job because of serious burn-out from doing two jobs at once. Just be sure that you can accept those terms before getting too excited about a job.

Figure 10.1

The Seven Tools HR Uses to Cut You

1. Clear, written instructions

2. The Yes/ No factor

3. Industry Knowledge

4. Annoyance

5. Relevance

6. Difficult communication

7. Gut reaction

Cut #1 – Clear, Written Instructions

What it is:
A long list of very specific instructions on how to apply for the job.

Why they do this:
If you can't follow clear, written instructions, HR does not want to talk to you.

How to pass:
Send them everything they ask for, in exactly the way they request it.

Kill Rate:
More than 50%

The first test in any application process is to see if you can follow clear, written instructions. The HR thought process is "if you can't follow written directions, I don't want to talk to you." Passing the test is simple – send them everything they ask for, in the way they tell you to send it. Seem simple enough? You would be shocked at how many people fail this test!

How to send it

Most commercial employment websites encourage you to use the "Apply Now" button to submit your resume. Read the ad carefully - there may be a secondary email address or link hiding in the job posting itself. In that case, send a separate email to that address. Check for a name as well; addressing the cover letter to the person shows that you are detail-oriented.

Should you use the "apply now" feature?

Yes - if there is no other option. Sometimes this is the only way to apply for the job. In cases where you find both an email and the "Apply Now," it is acceptable to do both. This does not create work for the HR department since they are the people who initiated this test in the first place.

Online applications

Some companies will re-direct the candidates to their website to fill out an online application, known as the Applicant Tracking System (ATS).

It can be time-consuming and tedious. However, it is necessary. This is definitely a test of your patience as much as your ability to fill out a form. Depending on the company, you may need to list every one of your skills, along with proficiency level. If you want to get past a computerized screening process, you must fill out those details.

Unfortunately, many people make mistakes in the online forms. One that people often miss involves uploading your Word document. The application system will scan your resume and fill in the information on their forms - a process known as "parsing." It is not uncommon for computers to incorrectly parse your resume. Take your time and double-check your work, correcting any false computer assumptions. If there are sections requiring lots of new information, type your answers in Word first; then copy and paste your answer after you perform spell-check.

Applicant Tracking Systems (ATS) are a horrible way to apply for a job. For this reason, they are often called the "HR Black Holes:"

resumes come in, but they don't go out. Computers are doing all the screening, and humans may not program them correctly. However, you can't skip this step. If you succeed in reaching the hiring manager but fail to fill out the online application, you can be cut for not follow instructions.

Most ATS screen candidates on job criteria alone. Unlike the major employment websites, you can only load up one resume on your user account. With this restriction, you can't use different resumes for different positions. To overcome this obstacle, you can create separate user accounts for the same company, making one for each target job. You will need to repeat the application/ uploading procedure for each one of the new accounts, which can be time consuming and frustrating. However, it may be worth your time if you want jobs in vastly different disciplines.

Another big problem with an ATS is user error - the HR recruiter, not yours. These systems are only as good as the person programming the results. Several years ago, a fellow recruiter told a horrifying story about their new ATS system. She had been using it for about three months when she noticed that all of their new hires had last names that started with A, B, C or D. As it turns out, she thought that her results from the ATS were showing her *ranked* candidates; in fact, it was giving her an *alphabetical list.*

If you run into an ATS, take three critical actions:

- Use a more general and universal form of your resume
- Contact HR to make sure your application was received
- Find another way to get to the hiring manager and send him the targeted resume

Cover letters: The unspoken standard
Some ads don't ask for a cover letter. *Send it anyway*. Always send a cover letter - it is standard business etiquette. It is expected, anticipated and necessary.

People who don't send a cover letter are seen as unprofessional and lazy. Even a bad cover letter that says, "Please see my attached resume. Thank you for your consideration" is better than nothing. Candidates who don't take the time to write a cover letter *always* get cut in early rounds of screening.

184

When applying online, consciously add your cover letter. The major sites call this "optional." Don't use the Quick Apply features from the major employment websites. Those do not send a cover letter with your resume. An ATS may or may not have a section for your cover letter. If it doesn't, you can add it to the top or bottom of your uploaded Word resume.

If you are emailing the HR department or the hiring manager directly, put your cover letter in the body of your email. You don't need to attach it separately. In fact, attaching a separate cover letter annoys the HR department - which is a violation of HR Rule #: Don't Annoy.

References

If they request references in the ad, send them. Writing "references available on request" on your resume does not count - everybody has references on request. If this requirement is in the ad, *they did request your references.*

You can include your references on your resume instead of using a separate document. Including references on the resume itself ensures that you won't forget them later. Moreover, adding them to the resume overcomes an ATS, which doesn't have a section for references - even when the company asks for references. If send your references as part of your resume, their delivery is guaranteed, no matter what the delivery method.

If you're nervous about confidentiality issues, put a stipulation directly on your reference sheet:

> *"As my employment search is confidential,*
> *please do not contact my references without*
> *my permission."*

This creates a legal responsibility on the employers' part. If they contact your references and it endangers your current job, they could be held liable.

However, no employer is going to take the time to contact your references before they at least do a phone interview with you. It is too time consuming. References are the *last step* in the employment process, not the first. Even recruitment agencies don't check references until they are certain of your abilities.

If unsolicited contact is still a concern for you, don't send the contact information. Just list the person's name, title and how they know you. Then add the statement: "contact information provided on request."

When sending references, be sure to send the right ones. Always include at least three professional references. If you have some personal ones to add as well, that's fine. If they know you in some sort of work capacity, such as volunteer work, that's even better. Listing only their name is not helpful either. Indicate their job title and how they know you. Other information, such as years known, is not required but it can be helpful. Long associations with others demonstrate your stability, which is a desirable trait to employers.

Salary history vs. salary requirements

Your salary history states how much you earned in each and every job. A Salary requirement states what you want in your next job.

If the job posting requests a salary history, should you send it? No!

A Great Truth

Never send your salary history when you apply for a job. Instead, state your salary range in your cover letter. This will deter job offers far below your target salary.

If you give your salary history, you just gave away your negotiation strength. Companies look at salary history to determine a salary offer. Many people change jobs to increase their salary by as little as 5-7%. If the employer knows the details of your past earnings, they may offer less based on your salary history.

On the other hand, you may be seeking considerably less. An employer may not believe you when they see the full salary history. You are cut because your desired salary doesn't seem logical to the HR person.

The only exception to the salary history rule is a professional salesperson, especially in commissioned positions. In that case, salary history is a reflection of success.

So how do you apply for a job posting with a salary history request?

What they really want to know is your *salary range*.

Salary range is a screening tool. Every job has a budget, whether that amount is listed in the job posting or not. Giving your salary range lets them know your expectations. If it is not within their ballpark, they won't ask you to play.

Using salary range for screening actually helps you. If you're honest and reasonable about your expectations, you would not want to consider a job out of your ballpark anyway. Too low won't fit your requirements - remember the exercise in Chapter 2, Defining Your Goals? Taking something below your minimum creates a losing situation for you. If the salary is way above your range, the employer's expectations may be above your abilities.

Express your salary range in the cover letter, not in the resume. This gives you the ability to adjust it for every job. Some positions are more demanding; asking for more money is reasonable. Other jobs may be on your own low end; maybe you are willing to make that monetary sacrifice temporarily to change careers or employers. Salary ranges in cover letters meets the HR screening requirements.

Salary range can be as large as $10,000 – your ideal salary should be closer to the lower end. For example, if your target salary were $45,000, an ideal range would be $43,000 - $50,000. Why? Two reasons: one, your bottom is never the bare minimum you can live on; and two, their ideal hire is in the middle of their range.

A Great Truth

In the salary game, the employer's don't want to hire the cheapest candidate. Their ideal salary is in the middle to higher end of their salary range. They want to hire the candidate who is the closest match for their needs without going over budget.

Figure 10-2: Salary range in the cover letter

Dear Mr. Smith:

How would you describe your ideal candidate for your Executive Assistant position listed on craigslist.com? Perhaps a detail-oriented professional, with proven problem solving skills and real-world experience? If so, I could be the candidate you seek.

In fact, I believe many aspects of my past eight years in the XYZ Industry would serve your needs extremely well.

My salary range is $51,000 to $58,000, with some flexibility considering benefits. As my employment search is confidential, please contact me on my cell phone, 303-555-1212. I would love for an opportunity to discuss your needs.

Sincerely,

Diligent Applicant

Salary history: A warning

Do be very cautious about sending your salary history. Unscrupulous characters do use job postings as a way to steal people's identities. Listing an attractive salary history could open the door to thieves. Check out the company's website before you send anything. At the very least, try to verify the email address. If a company's listing is completely confidential and you can't find any information about them, never send the salary history. If it is a legitimate job offering, wait for them to contact you before sending such a sensitive document.

IF you must send your salary history, make it a separate document. The format should follow your regular resume – jobs listed in same order and so on, - but with no duties or skills listed. This way, you will never mistake your salary history for your resume:

In Figure 10.3, the degree is included because it reflects the dramatic increase in salary. Same with the AR position: this applicant's increasing salary indicates positive work performance.

Figure 10.3: Properly formatted salary history

Serious Applicant
888 Fake St
Sometown, USA
333-555-9999

SALARY HISTORY:
Accountant, SomeCo, Denver, CO   Oct. 2005 - Present
        Current Salary: $60,000 annually

Accounts Receivable, So-N-So Company, Denver, CO   Jan. 2000 -
Oct 2005
        Final Salary: $ 51,000 annually
        Initial Salary: $35,000 annually

Accounting Assistant, So-N-So Company, Denver, CO May 1998 -
Jan. 2000
        Salary: $ 25,000

EDUCATION:
BA, University of Colorado, December 1999
        Major: Finance
    Graduate with Honors

Your fate is in your hands: follow the directions
Pay attention to every job ad. Some key instructions can be hiding in the job description for a reason. HR departments add extra steps or request extra materials on purpose. It is all a test.

* * *

Cut #2 - The Yes/ No Factor

What it is:
Specific criteria, skills, education or experience required to perform the job.

Why they do this:
They really do need this particular ability to succeed in this position.

How to pass:
Use the right key words and keep critical information easy to find.

Kill Rate:
Around 20%

Some criteria are a firm requirement in the mind of the employer. Maybe it is a critical skill for the job. Perhaps it is a specific college degree. If you are missing that crucial piece, you will be rejected. There is nothing you can do to change the employer's mind on a firm requirement.

It's a drop-dead, yes or no. You either have it or you don't.

If you think about it, some of these are obvious. For example, it is impossible to get a job as a registered nurse if you don't have a nursing degree. It is highly unlikely for you to land an executive assistant position if you have never worked in an administrative support role before. Nor will a gardener be hired as the vice president of sales, no matter how good his people skills are.

But don't lose heart yet - you can't tell from looking at the job description which requirement is a yes/no factor....

Don't have everything? Apply anyway!
Ever heard that before? It is true, and here's why: in every job description, some criteria matters more than others. You cannot tell which ones are the most important by reading the ad.

Some people try to put a formula to this, such as "the skill listed first is the most important," but that's just not true. For example, education requirements are frequently first, because *that is how traditional advertising is written.* The hiring manager may be more interested in the skill set or experience, but you would never know from reading the job posting.

Look at the assigned values for this job's Criteria Sheet. For this example, the criteria are listed in the same order as the job posting. In this case, the first three criteria are not the most important. Notice the ones with the least amount of value:

Figure 10.4: Criteria Sheet with points value

CRITERIA SHEET
Programming Technician
Total Points = 100

Points	Criteria
10	College Graduate
20	2 years of Broadcast industry experience
5	Must be available on-call during station broadcast hours
25	Ability to work with figures, especially on timing information
20	Prior experience with data entry
5	Familiarity with broadcasting operations and procedures
10	Ability to deal with a variety people with tact and efficiency
5	Must possess valid driver's license and be insurable through the company's insurance

In this real-world example, many people did not apply for this job because they didn't know broadcast operations or they were not available to be on-call. However, those two points were the ones that *mattered least.* The employers knew the new hire would need training, so they weighted the aptitude criteria heavier.

For every job, some criteria are more important than others. Don't screen yourself out. Apply to any job that captures your attention and leave the screening to the HR department.

Using the Key Element Detector™ for guidance

While you can't tell for sure what the drop-dead requirements are in a single job description, looking at a large sample can clue you in. If you keep seeing a criteria repeating in the Key Element Detector™, chances are that is an absolute. If you notice the exact same wording repeated in almost every ad, it is a serious the requirement.

For example, Human Resources jobs: unless a candidate carries a specific Human Resources degree with current certifications,

191

the career options are limited. Why? Laws are constantly changing, and a top HR Director must be extremely well versed in all the employment issues and changing requirements. Just as you wouldn't trust a surgeon without a license, a company will not trust their critical human resources functions to someone without a degree.

If you are serious about a career path and you know you are missing a critical degree, certification or skill, go get educated. With a complete Key Element Detector™, you have no excuse not to.

* * *

Cut #3 – Industry Knowledge

What it is:
Proper use of jargon, language, acronyms - this also includes grammar and spelling errors.

Why they do this:
This is the first test to see if you know what you're doing.

How to pass:
Check your work before sending any resume or cover letter. This includes reading it out loud to check the grammar and language.

Kill Rate:
5 - 10%

An uneducated or inexperienced candidate often misuses common industry jargon. Letters transposed in licensing acronyms, misinterpreted duties and badly written descriptions are all clues to the HR department. This is a sure-fire way to get cut. Nobody wants to put a sub-par candidate in front of the hiring manager; it reflects poorly on the HR department. Double-check your terminology to make sure you're on track and use your Key Element Detector™ to help verify your information.

If you are part of a highly technical or specialized industry, jargon becomes even more important. For example, I did some recruiting for the biodiesel industry - it's a renewable energy source that uses plant oils or animal fats to make diesel fuel for trucks and other vehicles. In searching for an engineer, we looked for someone who knew how to use the word "transesterfication." (It's the bio-chemical process that turns the fats into fuel, by the way.) Any engineer in biodiesel worth his salt knows what this means - which is why it was such a great screening term for us.

Grammar and spelling errors are death on any resume. It's even worse if you claim to be "detail oriented" and you misspell the company's name. Pay attention to the names of people in the target company; a misspelled name screams sloppy work. Look out for casual writing. While you want to sound human, being overly familiar can be offensive.

Even your documents need to have a professional title. Make sure they have your name and job title in the Word document name, such as "Jane Smith HR Director Resume.doc" instead of "Resume Draft 2.doc." HR departments receive literally hundreds of resumes every day. If your document doesn't include your name, chances are pretty high that it might get misplaced. And any error that occurs is your problem, not theirs.

The proper use of acronyms is very important. For example, one of my clients was a Certified Nursing Assistant (CNA), but on her resume, the spell check had corrected it to CAN. When we fixed this error, she began to get interviews the next week.

When using an acronym, be sure to write out the meaning and then the letters the first time the term is used - such as Applicant Tracking System (ATS). This is for two reasons: one, HR may not understand the acronym; and two, some companies will screen on the complete term instead of the acronym. That goes back to how well HR knows how to use its own ATS.

* * *

Cut #4 – Annoyance

What it is:
If you are annoying, HR will find an excuse to cut you.

Why they do this:
Three reasons: it can be a power trip, an easy cut or they just don't want to work with jerks.

How to pass:
Be clear and concise in all communications. Respect their time. Be professional at every turn.

Kill Rate:
5 - 10%

If you really get on the HR department's nerves, they will search through your resume to find the one mistake to cut you – or they may even invent one. At the screening level, HR people have a lot of power. Screening is conducted with minimal oversight, especially in the early rounds. In other words, they can cut you without fear of reprisal. This is even more reason for you to get directly in contact with the hiring manager. If he calls HR and tells them to look for your resume, his action trumps the screener.

No phone calls, please...
In most cases, the HR department does *not* mind if you call, as long as you are not pushy or annoying. Calling to verify information is acceptable, so long as you keep it minimal. You might call to verify that a position is open or what is their preferred resume format. However, don't call with the mindset that you want to find out specifics about the job. Some people use this excuse to "see if they want to apply." HR departments hate that. Apply first, and then make judgments about the company during an interview.

A Great Truth

The statement of "no phone calls, please" will discourage 90% of the applicants – which is what the HR department wants.

The best time to call is after you have emailed your resume. Ask three very specific questions:
1. Did you get my email?
2. Did you get the attached resume?
3. Are you able to open it and read it properly?

If they did not get it properly, be sure to ask what format would work best. Offer to send a hard copy as well, either delivered in person or in the mail. After you get those questions answered, you can ask other questions, but don't ask for an interview (that's very annoying). Don't show up at the office, resume in hand and expect someone from HR to come to the front desk to see you (that's even more annoying).

You do want to ask questions that relate to the HR person's job, such as volume of applicants. This works because people do enjoy talking about themselves.

Acceptable questions include:

1. Have you gotten a large response?
2. Will you be sending out notifications when the job closes?
3. When do they anticipate holding interviews?
4. Do you have other openings at your company?

If they are getting annoyed, be polite and end the call as soon as possible.

If you only get their voice mail, be courteous with your message, but don't expect them to call you back. A good department will still make note that you called.

Don't hound the HR department. If they don't return your phone call, be patient. They are probably very busy. Try following up with an email instead. Follow-through and making contact are positive traits, but don't call every day, nor should you send an email every day. It's ok to be interested, but don't let it slide into creepy stalking behavior.

ATS verification

You can call the HR department if you filled in the online application, just to make sure they received it. However, if you are having trouble with the system and want to get help, you will probably have minimal success. Many HR people don't want to walk you through the application; it's part of their test.

There may be something wrong with their system, such as a critical error. Treat this very carefully. HR hates calls that point out

195

flaws in their system. They know they have flaws; they just don't want to hear it from you.

Again, this is another reason why you don't want HR to control your fate. Get in touch with the hiring managers.

Multiple submissions

If a company has multiple openings, send a fresh resume and cover letter for each position, clearly stating the desired job. Saying, "please consider me for anything you feel I qualify for" is absolutely horrible. Guess what they think you're qualified for? Nothing. Be confident and tell them what you want. It's not their job to help you or to be your career counselor. It's their job to cut you.

Watch your mouth

Be careful about what you say to anyone in the company. Sounds obvious, right? You would be surprised at the number of people who get mouthy with the receptionist. Guess who talks to the receptionist? Hiring managers and HR. It's a common practice for the interviewers to ask the receptionist how you behaved in the lobby. Many front-runners have lost the job based on ill manners to the front desk.

A Great Truth

The receptionist is your doorway to the job offer or to the rejection pile.

Candidates can make fatal mistakes just by calling the main number in the wrong frame of mind. Frustrated callers have voiced their frustrations with HR to the receptionist, only to leave a sweet message on the recruiter's voice mail. The front desk and HR always communicates closely. A loudmouth candidate's resume will be tracked down to eliminate her from all future consideration - not just *that* job, but *all jobs.*

There really is a black list at every company. Make sure you don't end up on it.

Cut #5 – Relevance

What it is:
They are FINALLY reading your resume for content.

Why they do this:
NOW HR is looking for the right fit, not just cutting candidates.

How to pass:
Relevance applies to more than just the job posted. It includes your research on the company while emphasizing your strengths.

Acceptance Rate:
10%

By now you know the importance of using the right key terms and jargon. It cannot be stressed enough. If HR is scratching their heads trying to determine why you applied for a job, you lost.

Integrate your research about the company into your cover letter. Make sure your submitted materials stay on target to prove that you are the best candidate. Each and every job contains unique elements. A stock resume and cover letter may get you past the first level of screening, but that doesn't mean you will make the top 10%.

Believe it or not, but most candidates do not read the company's website before they apply. It is way too easy to just click on some old standards than to take 20 minutes to review the company itself. Taking even a few moments to customize a cover letter to the specific company shows your professionalism and thoroughness.

Remember, relevance is NOT about YOU - it is about the company's needs. Consider
- What challenges are in the industry?
- What problems can you solve?
- How can you generate or save money?

All of your extra work will rocket you into the final rounds.

* * *

Cut #6 – Difficult Communication

What it is:
If they have trouble reaching you, you may get cut.

Why they do this:
There are too many applicants. Due to short deadlines, they are just too busy to wait for you.

How to pass:
Answer your phone! If you can't do that, be professional and be responsive.

Kill Rate:
Depends on how good the competition is.

These are the lucky dogs who are actually getting called for a telephone interview. But that doesn't mean you're in the clear yet...

The screening process continues when the HR department starts calling candidates. One test involves how long it takes you to return their phone call. The top picks are called first, but if they have to leave a message, they do keep calling other candidates.

If you don't call back within a day, you might miss your chance. If they are really interested, they may call you again. However, no HR department will call the candidate a third time without a return phone call. At that point, they have moved on to someone who was more receptive.

In your cover letter, be sure to tell them the best number and time to call. This helps alleviate some of the communication barriers. However, action is required on your part to answer the calls.

Professional communication is more than just answering the phone. Often times, this is the first point where a recruiter notices that weird email address. I have seen recruiters move a candidate to the bottom of the pile because the email was suggestive or offensive.

Believe it or not, I have also seen candidates leave their phone number off of their resume. In some cases, it might be acceptable to leave your street address off and only include your city and state, but nobody hunts down the candidate who didn't provide a phone number. As a tip, be sure to include your full contact information in your cover

198

letter. This helps combat the problem of lost documents such as resumes.

Voice mail greets can be a major problem. All too often, a recruiter hears a message that starts with "hey, dude, I can't get the phone, but leave a message..." Or worse, some rap or heavy metal song. Another greeting recruiters hate is the "voice mail lady," with the generic message that only repeats the phone number called and not the name of the account holder.

Be sure to list your name on your greeting. Recruiters get antsy when they aren't sure about who they are talking to.

* * *

Cut #7 – Gut Reaction

What it is:
Before sending any candidate to the hiring manager, HR weights all of the factors. Those who have a positive experience move forward.

Why they do this:
Every candidate put before a hiring manager is a reflection of HR's work.

How to pass:
Be relevant, professional and passionate.

Pass Rate:
Only 3-5% of all applicants.

When the candidate list is narrowed to the top picks, instinct plays a part. The best HR recruiters and hiring managers often choose calling one candidate over another because "it feels right."

Hiring people is a risk, and employers are cautious. They want to feel confident in a person's abilities, even before they pick up the phone for the first contact. If you keep your materials professional, accurate and relevant, these subconscious feelings will react to your presentation. You appear to be someone who knows what they are doing. That's the instinct pull they are looking for; the ability to put them at ease.

All of the extra homework on researching the company pays off here. During your phone interview, be sure to ask relevant and intelligent questions.

Confidence comes across on paper. Self-respect is a tangible element in the job search, and it shows in the way you write and speak about yourself. Most employers want someone competent and interested in their specific job, not just "any old job". That's the "spark," the "magic bullet" to piece the corporate veils.

Finally, be sure to send a thank you note to the HR people for any interview - including a phone interview. While most candidates remember to thank a hiring manager, very few send thanks to a recruiter. This can help tip scales in your favor.

Be conscious of the tips and tricks HR uses to cut you and you will consistently be in the top 10%.

* * *

Final words on screening
Now that you know how the HR department is screening you, you never have to fall victim to these tricks. Remember to follow their rules, even the unsaid ones. Be professional and complete in all of your communications. Use your tools from this book to make sure you are in the top 10% of any candidate field.

Chapter 11 - Interview Tricks That Can Land the Job

It's no secret: few people enjoy interviewing. That goes double for hiring managers. On both sides of the table, interviews can be awkward, time-consuming and non-productive. Candidates are nervous and strained. Or worse, they spout what they think the hiring manager wants to hear. Hiring managers can be bored, distracted or even nervous themselves. Frequently, judgments are made on-the-spot and it can be hard to change that first impression.

Listening to the advice of professional job search advisor can drive you crazy. Some of the clichés don't even make sense, even as they are repeated in the job search community - does "turn your weakness into a strength" sound familiar? Then there are the "rules," which can be overwhelming: don't talk too much, don't say too little, don't wear black, don't talk about your personal life, and so on. It can be difficult to concentrate on the actual interview if you try to play by these rules.

Be Yourself, Be Honest - but Beware

I do not believe in putting up a "front" or a performance in an interview. It is more important to be yourself. Instead of forcing yourself to be something you're not, capitalize on what you have to offer.

A Great Truth

You don't need to be an extrovert to ace in an interview. Plenty of introverted, nervous or shy people are hired every day.

I have seen a lot of introverted or nervous people do worse in an interview because they are trying to operate out of their comfort zone. Instead of acknowledging their discomfort, they push themselves to be outgoing - which looks fake and forced to an interviewer.

Of course, it is important to practice and to know what you are going to say. However, it shouldn't be based on what some guy or internet article told you to do. If you can be yourself in an interview, you are more likely to get a job that is the right match for you - skills, duties and company culture fit.

Not to mention that many interviewers can tell when they are being snowballed.

Which brings up the next factor - be honest. It is okay for you to talk about your passions, your goals and your expectations. Honesty also extends to the difficult situations, such as being let go from a job. You need to reconcile your feelings about events like this before you get in the interview, so that you can talk about them with a positive mindset (see Chapter 7- Dealing with Discrepancies if you need help doing that).

If you do have an issue, it is best to mention it *when asked*, and then redirect with what you learned from the situation. HR just wants to make sure it is not a habit or a pattern. Notice that they have to ask first. In one interview, I had a candidate literally point to his conviction for a felony on his application. He explained that he had a cocaine issue in the past, but had sought treatment and was "all okay now!" While honest, not exactly the best way to make a good impression...

Finally, you need to beware. Don't let your brains fall on the floor. This is a competitive situation, and you do want to put your best foot forward.

"Beware" also means "be aware." Be aware of the interviewer, including body language, voice and what is not being said. If you only concentrate on your own performance, you miss the subtle clues which say tons about a working environment.

* * *

What Interviewers Really Want To Know

At every one of the interview phases, the employers want to know four basic questions:

1. Can you do the job?
This is all about the Technical Skills – do you have the ability to carry out the duties of the job? Depending on the demands of the job, this

can get very detailed. Be prepared to answer with actual examples from your experience.

2. Will you fit in?
These questions relate to personality, style and their corporate culture. Depending on the company or situation, this could be more or less important. Don't be fooled – even if they never ask questions down this path, they are making personal judgments based on your look, your actions and your reactions.

3. Do you have any issues?
Questions about your previous jobs can reveal more than simple experience. The interviewer could be fishing for your attitude about past employers. Are you blaming the company or former boss? Is your frustration shining through? What are your concerns in a workplace? Why do you have discrepancies in your work history?

4. Can I get you at the right price?
Some things are about the bottom line.

Depending on the interview stage, the questions will be emphasized differently...

Goals with each type of interview
Every phase of the employment cycle addresses specific objectives for the employers. Creating the job description identifies their needs. Screening candidates should reveal the top applicants. Each phases of interviewing accomplishes a goal as well:
Understanding their employer's goals puts some control back in your hands. For example, if you are undergoing a screening telephone interview, you don't need to go into deep explanations of past duties. If you are meeting the hiring manager the first time, concentrate on answering his questions in detail. When you are meeting the rest of the staff, relax; they think you might be the "right fit" for their team.

Figure 11.1: Goals for each interview

Stage	Conducted by...	Goal	How to Handle
Phone Interview	Lower level HR person	Screening on basics	• Schedule time, don't wing it • Have copy of job description • Don't gush - stick to facts
First Interview	HR department	Skills Fit Professionalism	• Dress for success • Bring copies of resume • Be prepared to answer technical questions • Have intelligent questions
Second Interview	Managers	Ability assessment Culture fit Negotiation feelers	• Tailor presentation to the person • Research them online beforehand • Higher level technical questions • Be personable
Subsequent interviews	Other managers, team members	Culture	• Be yourself, but cautious • Don't contradict earlier answers or images
Procedure Points	HR department	Checking references Legal requirements	• Be helpful
Job Offer	HR or Manager	Get you at the best price	• Be ready to negotiate

The phone interview: Technical abilities and price range

Phone interviews concern the "can you do the job" and "are you the right price" issues. A phone interview is first and foremost a screening tool. Lower-level employees conduct phone interviews and gauge your answers against the given qualifications. Screeners look for the technical proficiency required for the job. Their goal is to bring you in or cut you, a judgment made within 15 minutes or less.

You should always expect phone interview question like these:

1. <u>Are you still interested?</u>
   Hopefully, the screener will give you some more information about the job, or at least remind you of the open position. With multiple candidates, verifying availability is a priority for the employer. They don't want to waste time chasing uninterested candidates.

2. <u>Verification of your skill set</u>
   You will be asked about the skills listed on your resume. In addition to confirming the information, try to include an example, while still keeping the answer quick and to-the-point.

3. <u>Brief summary of why you're looking</u>
   Make sure you know how to answer this in a concise way, without pussy-footing around or bemoaning your situation. Develop a simple, clear answer for this question ahead of time. It is acceptable to mention you were laid off. Refrain from disclosing too many details to keep your own tone positive.

4. <u>What salary are you looking for?</u>
   As with your cover letter, speak only in terms of salary range. Naming your range is acceptable, but pining down a specific number at this point is not a good idea. If you aren't comfortable with stating a number first, ask the interviewer what *their* salary range is. You don't want to waste time chasing something below your goals.

   One variation on the salary question is when they asked what you were making in your last job. This may seem unfair, especially if your salary expectations have changed drastically (either up or down). When answering, you can point out that your circumstances have changed. Unfortunately, because you are dealing with an entry-level person at this point, they may push back harder for a firm answer. They don't have the authority or the knowledge to do otherwise.

Phone information you should pin down

Earning an interview is exciting. Don't let your enthusiasm blind your discretion. If at all possible, ask to call them back in 10 to 15 minutes, or suggest a scheduled interview time. You want to be in the right mindset for any interview, which means taking some time to prepare.

You need to stay focused during a phone interview to capture some screening information of your own. It will help with your pre-interview research later on. Keep your questions simple: the typical phone interview is only 15 minutes, and if you drag it out longer than this, you could be annoying the screener.

Be sure to take note of this critical information:

1. Verify the company, the job title and the interviewer's name
   Write it down. You can look up all of this information later. Don't take the time to conduct a quick internet search on the company while you're on the phone with someone. That is not proactive, it's rude.

2. Ask the basic nature of the job – even if you are holding the job description
   The screener knows the top attributes. Listen to his answers to figure out the focus of the job.

3. Where the company is located
   With internet job postings, you can't tell the location. Even local jobs might be across town and outside of your target area.

4. Their salary range
   In case they don't ask for yours, you should always ask for theirs. Again, speak in terms of range, not specifics. If it's not in your acceptable range, don't waste time pursuing this job further.

Salary games: "I'm sure they'll raise the salary for me!"

Some candidates will agree to any salary range on the phone, just to achieve the in-person interview. They believe that they can convince the hiring manager to raise the salary to meet their true target.

Don't play this game with employers. You may be able to raise the salary about their initial range, but expecting to drive the salary 20 - 30% more than the salary cap is unrealistic. Plus, it's extremely rude. Think about how much time of the employer's time you wasted by going through the entire interview process. Employers hate being blind-sided by sneaky salary games. You don't have to take their first offer, but at least be in the ballpark before you step up to the plate.

* * *

The first interview: In-depth technical skills and first impressions
Your first in-person interview is information gathering on both sides of the table. Employers will tell you more about the company and the expectations for the job. You will be sharing your experience and abilities. Conversation will turn to why you are interested in their job. You should project a desire to learn more about the opportunity.

At this point, you may be meeting another screening, either from HR or from the hiring manager's department. Either way, expect the technical questions again. This time, you can go into details and specific examples from your past. Brush up on those skills. Before the interview, write down some real-world examples to help you remember. Technical questions will comprise the majority of the first interview.

One of the first questions will be "Did you look at our website?" Don't miss this critical step! Failing to look at the website says, "I don't care about your company or your job." A five-minute perusal of their site can remind you about what draws you to the company. Develop your own questions - insightful, relevant and interesting questions shows your intelligence. Like your resume, the interview is not entirely about you. You are still trying to answer the employer's needs. You must be familiar with who they are and what they do.

You will be judged by the way you look; that's human nature. Next, people will listen to the *way* you say things. The very last piece considered is *what you actually said.* You want to exude professionalism in your clothes, your manner of speaking and lastly in your words.

Wearing a suit may not be mandatory for employees, but it is for the job interview. Look your professional best at the first interview – being too casual will cost you. Even in a traditionally casual industry, dress up for an interview. This conveys respect for the interviewer and your interest in the job. If the office is more casual, you can dress down some for the second interview. However, you really do get only one shot to make a positive first impression.

The only exception to the suit rule is if the company tells you what to wear. One major company would tell applicants to come to the interview wearing shorts. Anybody who didn't follow those specific instructions was cut.

Don't wear heavy fragrances (both men and women). Smells can turn negative very quickly in a closed office, and you never know who will be allergic to what. Sparkly or loud jewelry can be just as annoying.

Dress up your resume as well. Bring a printed copy with you, on a good resume stock. 24 lbs paper works well, but avoid card stock (60 lbs and higher). It gives people nasty paper cuts. Bring several copies, in case others sit in on the interview. Always have a copy for yourself.

While you may discuss salary ranges here, don't tip your hand to your final number. In fact, you should steer well away from salary or benefits discussions at all. Talking money early on shows that you only care about the cash.

* * *

The second interview: Personality and corporate culture
Congratulations – you are probably meeting the hiring manager at this point. Personality and culture are the keys here. You passed the technical skills assessment; sometimes you may have to take a formal test. The manager will ask you about those skills again, but pay attention to what she is saying about the job. Her real expectations may be different from the HR department's interpretation.

Keep the conversation evenly spaced. The hiring manager should speak 50% of the time or more. This allows you to get a feel for her priorities, style and attitude. You don't need to match the attitude; however, awareness can direct your answers. Be responsive to her questions.

Careful about the money discussions here – you don't want to negotiate salary *at any in-person interview.* Range is always acceptable, but don't low-ball yourself. The worst possible thing you can say is "I am seeking $50,000, but I'll take $45,000." Where do you think the offer will be?

True salary negotiations happen after the hiring manager has an opportunity to evaluate all of the candidates.

Subsequent interviews: The right fit

Most hiring decisions are made during the subsequent interviews. If you're working with management team, expect to come in a few more times to make sure you fit with everyone else. Third interviews are all about the corporate culture. Count yourself lucky if you get a chance to check out the team before making your decision.

* * *

The offer call

Let the negotiations begin! Unless the first salary offer is everything you've dreamed of, make a counter-offer. Very few people are comfortable asking for more salary, because they think the job offer will disappear. However, the offer will rarely be withdrawn if your counter-offer is reasonable. Conquer your fear and ask for a little more. Speak about money with confidence, not in vague statements like, "I was wondering if you would consider a slight increase."

If you need reasons to ask for more money, consider your skills and experience for this job. Willingness to take less in benefits and asking for more cash can work as well.

Keep it reasonable - you can play around within a few thousand dollars of the offer, but if you ask for 20% more salary, they won't play. And you look like a schmuck. Accepting interviews this far out of your target salary range is the ultimate in rudeness. It wastes your time, the interviewer's time and the hiring manager's time. The company has to go several steps back in the hiring process, slowing them down and costing them money and talent.

* * *

Interview the company: Develop your own questions

You always want to prepare your own questions. Every interviewer will ask, "Do you have any questions?" It is death to answer, "Uh, what are the benefits?" Be prepared and have intelligent questions relating to the company, the job and your own goals.

Your personal questions are *directly related* to your "Define Your Goals" exercises from Chapter 2. If advancement is important to you, be sure to ask the company about their promotions policy. If travel is what you seek, ask about the opportunity to see clients in person.

When developing your questions, consider these categories:

1. Fact-finding
   Facts cover everything from daily duties to department organization. It is the mechanics of the job and how you can perform them. Fact-finding covers the subtle layers that your research can't tell you.
   > *Examples: Who manages this position? What are the key responsibilities and duties? Has someone been in this position before? What did they do well? What did you dislike?*

2. Opportunity
   Find out as much as you can about the job itself. How does it fit with your goals? This could be confirming what you already know from your own research, but it's interesting to hear what the management says by comparison. On another level, these give you a chance to show off your research by asking related questions.
   > *Examples: Where do you see the company going in the next few years? I read about ___ industry challenge, how are you handling it? What is your marketing strategy for your new product line?*

3. Competition
   Ask about the company's hiring process. Find out where you stand without going off the deep end.
   > *Examples: Do you have many more interviews scheduled? When will you be making a final decision?*

What they don't want you to know
Want to avoid a control-freak or negative work situations? You had better ask some questions relating to this area.

While you can't ask "are you a screaming maniac?" Try these instead:

210

- How is your turnover rate?
  If their eyes wander the room while they hesitantly reply, "we had some people who weren't the right fit," look out.

- What is the biggest challenge in this job?
  Watching their body language tells you more than their words. If the biggest challenge is a control freak boss, the interviewer may hesitate or look away rather than offer a direct answer.

- Has this position been open for long?
  Difficult jobs are hard to fill and stay open longer. Or, conversely, the job has only been open for a week. That means the company is a meat grinder, crushing new employees who have to be replaced immediately.

If you're wary of a bad situation, pay attention to the people in the office. Are people jumping when the boss calls on the phone? Do they look strained and anxious? Can you cut the tension with a knife? Are you separated from the company's employees during the interview process? These are all bad signs – ignore them at your own peril.

* * *

Body language, room setup and territory
As with all human interaction, non-verbal communication is a vital element in interviews. Room arrangement reveals a specific message about the company. A cubicle-world environment with few personal affects is not supportive to the employees. A messy office can be signs of overwork; nobody has time to clean things.

When you arrive at the office, take some time to notice your surroundings. Talk to the receptionist. After all, the hiring manager will ask her how you acted in the lobby. When you are brought back for the interview, check out the room. Furniture set up can indicate the tone of the interview.

Watch their position with regard to you. Are they sitting higher than you are? Do they keep you standing too long? These are both power plays to make you uncomfortable or to put them in a superior positioning.

If you're seated directly across the desk from them, this is another power position – with you as the bug under the microscope. Chairs placed off the side or a desk or at 45 degrees are more casual and comfortable. Try to position yourself at a right angle to them, whether at a desk or in a conference room. It's less confrontational.

Body language says a lot. Someone who has their arms crossed over their chest is practically radiating a closed mind. If their hands are behind their head, they are mentally out-to-lunch or completely self-absorbed. Or worse, it is an aggressive move; think of animals trying to puff themselves up to look bigger, and you get the idea.

Notice the position of their hands. Do they cover their mouth with their hands, or are their hands under their chin? These movements convey inward reflection. It may not be bad; they could be more introspective, and this gives them physical distance to consider things. Interested people tend to lean forward; their hand gestures tend to move in your direction, as if they are reaching out to you.

* * *

Suggestions for you
Use a firm, normal handshake. Maintain eye contact and remember to blink. Sit comfortably in the chair, but not all the way back. You should be more forward, showing your interest in what the interviewer is saying. You want to keep the contact open. If you talk with your hands, don't let them fly all over the place. In that case, try to restrain more by keep your hands in your lap. What you think are minimal movements tend to be exaggerated in stressful situations.

If you're introverted by nature, that is perfectly okay. A big myth in job searching is that only outgoing, gregarious people do well in interviews, and therefore they are the ones getting hired. Truth is, being comfortable with yourself conveys a lot more than being overly bold. Don't chastise yourself. Find a way to make your nature work for you. For example, taking time to answer questions shows thoughtfulness, not weakness.

What not to do:
1. Don't put anything on their desk - this is crossing boundaries
2. Don't chew gum or anything else

3. Don't lose your sense of humor
4. Don't smoke beforehand
5. Make sure you say their name at least once
6. While chemistry is important in an interview, but it is not the only factor. If rapport or a genuine connection is not there, don't give up - it may not be as bad as you think.

* * *

Handling Different Interviewer Styles

Employers try all kinds of different tactics for interviews. Some will subject you to a veritable stress test, just to see how you react. Or they may act friendly, setting you at ease so that you reveal more than originally intended.

However, not every interviewer is a polished interview expert. The manager may be just as nervous as you. Or they may have horrible people skills. In any case, anticipating these various styles and knowing how to deal with them can help you ace even the worst interview situation.

Friendly and Personable

Don't be fooled! By being open and nice, the interviewer is putting you at ease, getting you lower your guard. In truth, she is evaluating everything you say. Candidates will reveal more in a relaxed atmosphere. Ever come out of an interview convinced you're hired because you "really connected" – only to be shocked when you didn't get the job? You were taken in by the Friendly Style.

Survival Tactic:
Don't get too comfortable. Stay on your toes and keep your goals in mind.

Figure 11.2: Different interviewer styles

Name	Traits	Mentality	Survival Tactic
Friendly and Personable	Nice, interested in you, engaged, relaxed and understanding	Get you relaxed to reveal more than you intended	Stay on your toes
Nervous and Uncomfortable	Rambling, may forget to ask questions, jumpy	They really are nervous!	Take control
The Skeptic	Reserved, distant, distrustful, cold	Possible bad experience in the past that they don't want to repeat OR expectation that it's your job to impress them	Be thorough and don't take personally
Bored and boring	Lethargic, listless, yawns, blank expression	Having a bad day, just back from lunch or not feeling well	Speed up pace and intensity
The Introvert	Quiet, reserved, calm	Is present, just not flamboyant	Don't overload
By the Book	Sticks to procedure, won't deviate from questions, methodical	Method is form of control OR tight screening requirements OR secret introvert	Let them have their process - give time to write answers
Surreal	Odd questions	Thinks they will reveal how your mind works	Your thought process matters
Highly Technical	Very detailed questions, unforgiving attitude	Really expects you to know this	Study beforehand
Deliberately Confrontational	"I'm gonna getcha!" Dismissive, cuts you off, drills into answers	Pressure test OR thinks he's an excellent judge of character	Breathe and stay calm

Nervous and Uncomfortable

This is not an act! Not all hiring managers are smooth and polished. The interview process can intimidate them as well. If he tends to ramble on about the job and forget to ask questions, he's stumbling through it. Likewise, his questions may be very terse and limited. Body language is a clear give-away here. Nervous interviewers make less eye contact, may pour over the resume and may even be hunched in their chair. It is possible to engage them, but don't overpower.

> **Survival Tactic:**
> *Take the lead. Offer to tell him about your experience and skills. Be proactive with your questions. Ask him what he did or didn't like about the last person in the job. Be sure to ask what his expectations are going forward.*

The Skeptic

Here's the grumpy interviewer. Everything about her manner is reserved and distant. Arms crossed, she doesn't seem to believe anything you're saying. Why? There are a couple of reasons for this attitude. First, somebody let her down before. Whether it was the person they just let go or a bad employee from a year ago, she does not want to make the same mistake twice. As a result, she is hard to deal with in the interview. Second, she may be expecting you to sell yourself. By limiting the non-verbal communication, she hopes that you will not react to subtle clues as to what she's looking for. It's a way to de-rail candidates from saying what she wants to hear.

> **Survival Tactic:**
> *Drop the touchy-feely answers and use solid examples of your accomplishments. Maintain your good humor and self-confidence. Remember, she's trying to rattle you by acting cold.*

The Bored and the Boring

This interviewer may seem completely withdrawn. He could look lethargic, listless or just plain bored. You could be his fourth interview of the day, or coming in just after lunch when productivity lags. Everything says he's just not into you (yawn.) However, be careful; don't mistake an introvert for boredom.

> **Survival Tactic:**

Be concise and get to the point. Show your own enthusiasm for the job. Ask him about himself. People like to talk about themselves, and this could bring him into your conversation.

The Introvert

The Introvert appears reserved and distant, but not to the degree of the Skeptic. He tends to sit back in his chair during an interview - not because he isn't engaged, but because he is taking everything in. Introverts tend to cover their mouths when they are thinking. Another clear indication is when he looks away to think about something you just said. This is a process of internalization, especially if the eyes shift up. On the whole, Introverts are quiet, calm and very, very sharp.

Survival Tactic:
Unlike the Bored interviewer, showing too much enthusiasm can overwhelm the Introvert. Overloading him can be taken almost as a threat, and certainly is a major culture clash. Instead, match the pacing and body language of the interviewer to build nonverbal rapport.

By The Book

This is a process-driven person. She has her list of questions and she's sticking to them no matter what. Often times, she tries to write down your answers during the interview. So what is up with that? Her position in the company can give a clue as to her motive. For example, if she's from the HR department or someone's assistant, she's running you through the screening process. A manager who uses this tactic is a process-driven person, methodical in everything she does. Or she might be using her prepared questions to hide her own introverted nature.

Survival Tactic:
Let her have her process. Answer questions fully, but give her time to write her answers. It is actually a big pet peeve if you keep talking while she's writing. After all, she can't stop writing until you stop answering the question! This is an efficient person and expects people to get to the point. Stay on her agenda and follow her methodology.

Surreal

Not too long ago, an interviewing fad hit the internet: throw bizarre questions at candidates to see how they think. "How many quarters does it take to reach the top of the Empire State Building?" "If you lined up hamsters nose to tail, how many would it take to reach the moon?" "How would you sort a bucket of golf balls?" All this goofiness was supposed to give insight into your problem-solving skills. In practice, it's just weird and few managers do this anymore. On the other hand, progressive companies like Google use logic tests to weed out candidates. In that case, you DO need the right answer to move forward in the process.

> ***Survival Tactic:***
> *Think before you answer. The actual answer doesn't matter. These questions give insight into your thinking process and flexibility.*

Highly Technical

If you are going after a very technical job, be prepared for this type of interviewer. You may encounter very specific and detailed questions to test your knowledge. Timed and graded skills tests could be part of the assessment.

One engineer I know interviews all the new PhD candidates for a Research & Design company. He grilled them on specific formulas and principles for over an hour. If an applicant didn't know the exact definition and application of entropy, he would get marked down – and saw the marks being made on his resume. (In advanced physics, entropy is an exact mathematical equation, in case you didn't know.) Candidates left the office feeling like they just took the worst college exam of their lives. Certainly, it was the most grueling interview they would ever encounter. However, people did get hired; just because a test is tough doesn't mean you lost the opportunity.

> ***Survival Tactic:***
> *Think before you answer. If you're struggling with an answer, don't let it rattle you too badly. Prepare for this interview: study up on key points, skills or processes necessary for your job.*

Deliberately Confrontational

For some reason, top executives tend to favor this type of interview style because they think they are an "excellent judge of character." Everything about this interviewer's attitude screams "I'm gonna get ya!" He is dismissive, he cuts you off, he drills into your answers with an air of scorn. Why? He wants to see how you act under pressure. Don't worry; he may not be like this in the workplace. Often times he will be a completely different person on the second interview. His philosophy is to see you sweat in the interview; that way, he knows you can handle the job.

> ***Survival tactic:***
> *Don't forget to breathe! Get grounded and stay focused. Don't give in to the stress or get upset. It will be over soon!*

* * *

Multiple person interviews

In some cases, you will interview with more than one person. Panel interviews make the most of everyone's time. You will normally be notified about a panel interview ahead of time. If not, don't be scared. Just roll with the punches. Part of the test is seeing how you handle the stress and adapt to unexpected situations.

Panels can be combinations of several interview styles, with each person taking a different role. After the interview, the panel members compare notes, sharing their impressions from different points of view.

Good Cop / Bad Cop

Yes, it's cheesy as hell, but some people watch too much TV. It's really a combination of a Friendly style interviewer with the Confrontational.

> ***Survival Tactic:***
> *Remember, this set up is an act. Deal with each interviewer in a consistent manner. They are looking for the conflicting answers.*

Figure 11.3: Multiple interviewer styles

Name	Traits	Mentality	Survival Tactic
Good Cop/ Bad Cop	A friendly with a confrontational style	Designed to cross-examine and see your reactions to stress	Don't cave to pressure
Redirection	Only one person in the room asks questions – but who is really in control?	Gauging your social skills, hiding authority so you won't focus on them (genuine reactions)	Address both equally
Panel	Varies: could have one main questioner or they may share the duties. Could have combinations of all previous styles.	Timesaver, committee opinion, methodical and reserved	Good eye contact across the panel

Redirection

If two people are in the room, who is the boss? Are you sure? They may even throw conflicting body language. One could be checking his email while the other is a very engaging conversationalist. Be sure to address *both*. This is a power play on their part, seeing if you can keep it straight.

> ***Survival Tactic****:*
> *Stay focused on the principal, or the one with the authority. If you aren't sure who it is, address both equally, even if one is ignoring you. He is there for a reason. It is acceptable to ask questions about who would be your direct supervisor.*

Panel Interviews

Some companies use panel interviews as a matter of policy. Only one person may ask the questions, or they may take turns. You could easily run into all the individual interviewer styles. However, the panel itself is not designed to "get you." It is ultimately a time saver for the company, allowing for multiple opinions of all the candidates in one meeting.

Survival Tactic:
Address your answers to everyone. Make eye contact at least twice with every member. Don't forget to breathe and keep your sense of humor.

No matter how many interviewer styles you encounter, try to keep your own cool. Notice your own personal style of interviewing: are you nervous? Are you friendlier? Are you withdrawn? Try practicing with others to see where your own abilities fall. From there, you can learn to adapt to any interview situation.

* * *

"So tell us a bit about yourself!"

What is the first question at almost every interview? "Tell us about yourself!" Believe it or not, a shocking number of candidates don't know how to answer this question.

No matter what approach you use, your introduction should not be more than 30 seconds long. Hitting this mark saves you from rambling, or from saying too little. Next, repeat your name. I know what you're thinking: "They already know my name. It's on my resume!"

People commonly forget names. Your interviewer may be meeting 10 or even 15 different people for this job. You want to use any and all tricks to be remembered. Saying your name gives them a chance to hear it as well as read it.

Overall, you want to engage as many of the interviewer's senses as possible. Let them hear your name to engage their auditory senses. Hit the visual learners by looking nice and presentable. Hand them a resume or business card to make them touch a physical object. Be sure to touch them in some way. Your handshake should be warm and inviting, not crushing, cold or clammy. Smell nice and clean, not dripping with heavy scents.

Your intention is to build a personal connection with the interviewer. However, this won't happen automatically. Prepare your introduction beforehand. Knowing how you will start your interview will reduce your own nervousness. It keeps you focused and more comfortable, and helps you speak comfortably about yourself.

Prepare a few different variations to handle different situations. For example, a fast-paced office will require a high impact introduction. A more casual environment needs a warmer introduction. If the interviewer looks harried or distracted, get to the point right away to make the most of her time.

Four common introduction formats are an elevator speech, a location-based introduction, a personal beliefs introduction or an interesting event introduction.

The elevator speech

During an elevator speech, you run down your top qualifications experience and skills in 30 seconds. Conclude with your interest in the position. The name "elevator speech" derives from the concept of how would you intrigue a stranger in your business skills during an average elevator ride. The technique works well if you are interviewing for a sales position or any job where you have to make an impression in a short period of time.

Figure 11.4: Elevator speech introduction

Interviewer: Tell me a little bit about yourself.

Candidate: Well, my name is Henry Jones, and for the last ten years, I've been working in software sales. My specialty is securing large businesses for telephony products to connect offices across the country. I've sold multi-million dollar contracts to Fortune 500 companies, saving them millions in lost man-hours. I'm looking to move into sales management, where I can teach junior sales reps my effective techniques, while still working directly with clients myself.

Interviewer: Very well. We are a solutions-based company ourselves, which sounds like your experience.

My Elevator Speech:

_____

_____

Little tough coming up with it based on those instructions, isn't it?

Instead of relying on a dry elevator speech with vague definitions, it is easier to use a focal point. The focal point can be almost anything that relates to your career: is it a skill set, or your past experience? Do you have special training that pertains to their needs?

To build a better elevator speech, use <u>JUST ONE</u> of the focal points:

Key achievement from my last job:

_____

I just finished:

_____

In my past job, I was known for:

_____

My career goal is:

_____

While you're still trying to determine your best elevator speech, brainstorm possible answers for each of the focal points. The more writing you do, you move closer to the truth about yourself.

* * *

The location-based introduction

How often have you met someone and asked where they're from? People like to talk geography. It is an easy way to relate to others because of the shared experience, in travel, background, culture or impressions. It's part of natural conversation, and a natural way to build rapport.

Figure 11.5: Location-based introduction

Candidate: My name is Bob Smith, and I'm originally from Texas, although I've been living in Denver for three years.

Interviewer: Really? What part of Texas?

Candidate: In the Dallas area.

Interviewer: I have family in Houston. Do you ever get back there?

Candidate: When I'm able. I've been to Houston as well. It's a great city.

Interviewer: I enjoy getting back home every now and then too. Anyways, let me tell you more about this job...

You can expand with more information about your location, such as adding your favorite sports team or mentioning your college. Location introductions work well in more casual environments.

Consider these factors to develop your location introduction:

Where I live now:

_____

Where I am from originally:

_____

Why I moved

_____

My favorite sports team:

_____

Where I went to school.:

_____

Only pick one or two of the factors. Trying to add more than this will distract from your main goal of the introduction: developing natural conversation about the job opportunity.

* * *

Interesting event introduction

If you've been doing something unusual in your recent past, you can address this as well. An interesting event can stay with the interviewer long after the interview, making sure you are remembers. However, the other half of this introduction must stress your interest in this particular job. You must present a well-rounded impression, or the event will work against you.

Your introduction doesn't have to be a showstopper, but it should sound natural and comfortable. Volunteer work can be an impressive introduction, but stay clear from anything controversial or that implies a protected affiliation, such as religious organizations. Hobbies that tie to your work experience or show positive characteristics are pure gold. For example, I am a second-degree black belt. In the interview situation, this shows personal discipline and commitment.

In this situation, the candidate talks openly about a lapse in his work history, while giving a unique insight into his character:

Figure 11.6: interesting event introduction

Candidate: I'm Dan Smith. I'm actually getting back to full time sales work after taking some time to help my son train for a pro baseball career. He's with a minor league team now, and I'm ready to get back to doing software sales.

Interviewer: Wow, that's great. What team is he with?

Candidate: He's with the Sky Sox, which is the feeder team for the Rockies.

Interviewer: What position does he play?

Candidate: He's an outfielder, with a really solid batting average.

Interviewer: I'm sure he must be, to start a professional career.

Candidate: I was fortunate that I could take the time to coach him. Now I'm ready to give my next employer that same kind of commitment.

Interviewer: Then let's talk about what we're looking for...

Do be careful about events that pull away from this job. For example, statements like "I am interested in your accounting job, but my real passion is writing. I'm hoping to sell my first book soon." To an interviewer, this says you don't really want my job at all.

Consideration for the interesting event introductions:

People wouldn't guess that I:

_____

I'm proud of:

_____

My favorite industry-related subject in school:

_____

My passion or hobby is

_____

* * *

The Passion Statement introduction

Remember your Passion Statement that we created for your resume? You can use this as the base for your interview introduction as well. If you are interviewing for a job that means a lot to you personally, those convictions can be a great way to start the interview. This method is very effective in any company with a strong mission statement, such as

225

non-profits, research & design focused jobs and socially conscious businesses.

More than any other introduction, the Passion Statement follows a specific format:

Always start with:

Why am I interested in this industry/ company:

_____

Then continue to expand with <u>one</u> of these:

What I have done to pursue this cause:

_____

What their mission means to me:

_____

Education that relates to this industry:

_____

How I want to make a difference:

_____

Employers want to hire people who are excited about their company, which is what the personal beliefs introduction highlights.

To make the Passion Statement effective, be sure to review the company's own commitment to their mission statement before the interview. Are they walking their talk? Can you find recent news that supports the company's beliefs? Mentioning these during the interview shows not only your research skills and commitment, but also how you are aligned with their beliefs.

Figure 11.7: Passion Statement Introduction

> Candidate: My name is Jane Smith. I'm actually very excited to interview with XYZ Solar Panels because I studied the effects of emerging green industries while I was in college.
>
> Interviewer: What drew you to the renewable energies?
>
> Candidate: Ever since I was a kid, I've been conscious of environmental issues. When I went to college, I specifically chose EcoTech for their curriculum in the renewable energies field. Now that I've graduated, I am eager to put that knowledge to good use.
>
> Interviewer: Well, good. We like passion for our cause. Let me tell you more about our company...

* * *

Develop your own introduction

Try playing around with the four different introductions. Write out a few different variations on each of the styles. Practice your opening statements aloud to hear the rhythm and honesty in each one. Practice them until they sound polished, but not canned. Get your friends and family to critique your performance.

In the end, your introduction should come naturally and put you at ease. In many ways, a well-executed introduction provides strength against your own nerves. It is a tool for you more than anything else.

* * *

Handling Difficult Interview Questions

While you can't anticipate every single question that will be asked in an interview, you can prepare for some of the most difficult ones.

In this section, we take a look at some of the most dreaded interview questions out there. My goal is not to give you stock answers that will work in any given situation. If you want that, Google common interview questions.

Instead, I want you to use these hated questions to do a bit of soul-searching. Remember, our goal is to be honest, be yourself and be aware. Getting to that stage requires some work on your part.

Doing the work

For each one of these interview questions, brainstorm at least three answers for each of these questions. Don't limit any answer- in fact, include at least one goofy answer - such as your greatest weakness is chocolate or shopping for shoes. Some of the answers that surface may be brutally honest, like your greatest weakness is how you handle conflict or stress. Whatever comes to mind just let it flow from your brain to your pen.

If you do enough writing, the honest and true answer will become apparent.

THEN you get to apply your "beware" filter. While some answers may be 100% true, it may not be the best answer in an interview situation. For example, you would never say "my greatest weakness is that I am late to everything." Nobody wants to hire someone who is chronically late! Just file that one away as something that you need to work on...

The best answers are the ones that are believable in addition to being honest. Years ago while I was developing these interview techniques, I did the soul-searching to find my weaknesses. What came out on top was the fact that I don't self promote in work situations. I am not the kind of person who toots her own horn to the boss, letting her know all the wonderful extras that I did for the company every day. My co-workers knew, because I would constantly ask if I could help them out. However, the boss never saw that, and I actually got marked down on a performance review because she didn't know all of the team work I took on. So for me, self-promotion was a real problem. But here's the rub: that answer doesn't work in an interview situation. After spending 30 minutes talking about how great I was, nobody believed that I didn't self-promote. While it was a brilliant and real answer, it was completely unbelievable.

Don't be satisfied with the first answer. Dig deep to get more options, just in case your first instincts need to be adjusted.

The most dreaded question of all time: "What is your greatest weakness?"
The common advice for this question is to "take a weakness and make it strength." This example shows the theory in action:

> *"I have a tendency to take on a lot of things, but I keep detailed checklists to get everything done. So even though I may have trouble saying no, I am always sure to handle everything on my list. That, and I know how to prioritize, so even though I take on a lot, I always hit my deadlines. So that is why my greatest weakness is saying no, but it doesn't really hold me back because I can always adjust my schedules and work load to hit the right deadlines..."*

This answer is an example of "tap-dancing." Under the stress of the interview, candidates start to ramble, trying to bring the negative trait around to a positive spin. This sounds exactly like what it is - a bunch of malarkey. It is not a position of strength; it comes across as a verbal dodge and interviewers hate it. The only thing worse is "uh, I can't think of any weaknesses."

A Great Truth

Every career has a typical greatest weakness, and experienced interviewers expect those answers. What they really want to know is *how you handle* your weaknesses.

For example, wonderful salesmen are frequently dislike paperwork because they are focused on people skills, not administrative functions. Good administrative assistants have trouble saying "no" to extra projects because they are, by nature, supportive team players. Accountants tend to be perfectionist because they need to be thorough and exact in their work.

The strongest way to answer this question is to be honest about your weakness. This shows introspection and personal understanding. What is most important is *how you manage* this weakness. That is what the interviewer really wants to know, not some trumped-up statement that tries to turn that fault into an asset.

Think of areas you need to improve. Are you more of a people-person, a process-person or a results-person? If you understand your own work and communication styles, you can easily identify the weaknesses as well as the strengths.

What is your greatest weakness?

_____

_____

_____

_____

Answers interviewers hate: *"I can't think of any;" tap dancing to "turn a weakness into strength."*

* * *

Future planning: "Where do you see yourself in five years?"
The "five year plan" question is a traditional question, but the right response has changed. In corporate America 30 years ago, the appropriate answer would be to get in with a company, steadily moving up the ladder and establishing a long-term career with one employer. It was common and desirable to stay with one employer for 10, 20 or even 30 years.

However, in the recession in the 1980's, this employment model was shattered by the employers. Rather than reward longevity, companies would lay off the most experienced workers to hire cheaper, entry-level employees. They stopped investing in their work force training, because it was so much easier to get someone who already had those skills. What was once a 20-year long job turned into 5 years, if the new hire was lucky.

By the time Generation X entered the workforce in the 1990's, work attitudes shifted again. Employees now act like "free agents," changing their work situation to move ahead or to get better salary offers.

Currently, typical time in one job is three years. HR now perceives people who stay in one job for more than five years as non-ambitious. The average Generation X worker will change his *career* – not just his job, but his entire *career* – at least three times. Generation Y (aka the Millennials) are even more non-traditional, seeking unique career pathways that capitalize on the changing markets. Building a career through multiple jobs or consulting work is now routine.

So what's the right answer to this five year plan? The one that honestly matches your career path. If your professional pattern is to move up the corporate ladder at one company, it is logical for you to seek the same now. If you need constant challenge and professional growth, your goal is to promote your career and follow the best opportunities. Maybe you do want to be in the same job, doing what you love. Phrase your answer that way.

When brainstorming, consider your real goals, both personally and professionally. Some personal goals you would not admit in an interview, such as wanting to start a family. Nevertheless, write them down now to help formulate what is an acceptable work situation to you.

One warning: if you are pursuing two different careers, don't mention this to the interviewer. A statement like "I want to work as an Office Manager until my singing career hits" says that you aren't serious about this job. Another problem is "I am considering several career paths right now, and depending on the job I get, that's where I'll focus my efforts." This looks uncommitted, plus managers want to hire somebody excited about the job.

Keep your goal honest, but it must be relevant to the current job discussion.

Where do you see yourself five years from now?

_____

_____

_____

_____

Answers interviewers hate: Saying what you think we want to hear; vague or unarticulated ideas; irrelevant goals; "I want your job!" (The last one is not clever; it's threatening.)

* * *

Your opinion of the boss and your co-workers: "What kind of person do you find the most difficult to work with?"
If you are like most people, you just screamed "Control freaks and micro-managers!" However, you can't say that in an interview. It brings questions about your ability to work for a demanding person. And, of course, no micromanager thinks that he is one; he just has "high standards."

You need to understand the *why* of control freaks before you can answer this question. Two things drive control freaks: fear and mistrust. They fear being taken advantage of. They fear shoddy results. They fear letting go of their pet projects because someone let them down in the past - that can be a real or an imagined truth. They don't trust others to do something as well as they can, so they create systems to double-check their employees' work.

If control freaks drive you nuts, phrase your answer as "I don't like it when my boss doesn't trust me to do the job the way she trained me. I am always open to suggestions, and like to earn her trust by doing the best I can." This satisfies most interviewers because it is insightful and honest, without being threatening or evasive.

If your main issue is other employees, be careful about falling into blame-games. Even if a previous co-worker shirked his responsibilities, find a way to stay positive in your statements. Instead of "I hate it when co-workers dump their work on me," try "While I enjoy being a team player and helping out my co-workers, it bothers me when others don't take responsible for their own workload."

One big tip: *NEVER speak badly about a past employer.* No matter what the situation - do not ever complain about a past employer. Anytime you get negative - even if it's not your fault - it looks bad on you. Once you start on a negative path, your attitude and answers spiral downward. Not to mention that you look whiny...

Like the "greatest weakness" question, employers want to know *how you deal with difficult people.* When brainstorming your answers, consider your coping mechanisms as well. Be honest; if you blow off steam by complaining to other employees, this is not a positive outlet. In an interview, you would not mention your negative coping mechanisms. However, you need to be aware of your own tendencies. Re-evaluate your own methods to identify more positive approaches.

What type of person do you find most difficult to work with?

_____

_____

_____

_____

Answers interviewers hate: Complaining or blaming others; "I get along with everybody!"

* * *

Finding out your dislikes: "What things frustrate you the most?" The answers to this question can be people-centered, management-centered or task-centered. Unlike the difficult people question, this question reveals what you don't like to do in your job. Where are your buttons? Is some critical function of the job one of your least favorite things to do? If so, they probably won't hire you.

As with all of these questions, employers want to know *how you deal with the situation.* The best answers revolve around one particular situation and scenario, followed by your solution to the problem. For example, a salesman who is frustrated with paperwork may set up a discipline to fill out the forms with the customer to capture vital information. In this manner, his frustration becomes a tool to stay focused.

When brainstorming these answers, consider all three aspects: people you've worked with, management you've questioned and duties that drove you nuts. Is there a recurring theme? If so, you might want to be aware of these issues in the job interview. Can you pick up clues from the interviewer about unacceptable situations?

While this exercise may bring many negative responses, guide your final answer around a situation that did have a good outcome or one that encouraged you to grow professionally.

What things frustrate you the most? How do you cope with them?

_____

_____

_____

_____

> *Answers interviewers hate:* Complaining. Creating a list of
> only negative responses, without mentioning how the
> issue was handled.

* * *

Overcoming difficulties: "What are some past work experiences (or problems) that you would hope to avoid in the future and why?"
It may seem like we've already covered this issue. Not so. While a frustration may be workable, experiences you hope to avoid gives insight into your boundaries, standards and professionalism.

An insightful manager knows the problems are in her department. She is looking for someone who can solve the problem. However, some problems are unsolvable. In that case, she needs someone who can work in her environment without getting so discouraged that he quits.

Answers need to be thought-out. In addition to identifying the problem, come up with a positive result. The situation may not have been solved, but you should have some professional or personal growth from the situation. For example, sometimes the best answer is to leave a company, without laying blame or acting like a victim.

This question can also be related to the company culture. Once, I was hiring a new administrative assistant. When I asked her about situations she wanted to avoid, she said "I really don't like foul language in the workplace. It is just very unprofessional." Well, at this company, crude language was often the norm. While the candidate's skills and experience were superior, she would have hated this work environment.

Always avoid negative answers or complaining. It doesn't matter if your former boss really was a screaming egomaniac. The moment you focus on bad situations, you attitude starts a downward spiral. This creates a very negative impression with the interviewer. This is why you must reconcile your feelings about the past before you can move on.

What are some past work experiences (or problems) that you would hope to avoid in the future and why?

_____

_____

_____

_____

Answers they hate: *Avoiding the question; victim mentality; complaining or blaming others.*

* * *

Your final pitch: "Why should we hire you?"
Some interviewers want to end with a hard-core sales pitch. They are expecting you to present a real strength that sets you apart from everyone else they've interviewed.

I will give you the right answer to this question – it is not your technical skills! Everyone at the interview stage has a similar skill set. Otherwise, they would not have gotten this far in the hiring process. Touch on your abilities, but that's not your final selling point.

It might have something to do with your experience, but even that is not the main factor. If you have unique experience to their industry, highlight this, but there is more to you than just your work history.

What sets you aside from every other candidate is your personality. No one is exactly like you. Determination, professionalism, grace-under-fire: have you demonstrated these attributes throughout the job interview? Are you helpful and supportive? Did you bring up examples? What is your best trait as an employee? How about as a person?

Your final pitch is a summary of one or two top skills or abilities, plus a reiteration of your unique self. All good presentations follow the same pattern: tell them what you are going to say, tell them, and then remind them of what you just said. Add some of your own self to this. Always remember, employers hire *people, not just skill sets.*

Why should we hire you? (*Or the more tactful*) If hired, what could you contribute that the other candidates could not?

_____

_____

_____

_____

Answers they hate: boring repetition of your resume or a lack of preparation.

* * *

Oh, I wish I had said that!
So you totally blew a question. Ever get in your car and think of a dozen better answers to a tough question? Unfortunately, you can't repair the damage you just did, but you can avoid the pitfall in the future. When you get home, write down that tough question and all of your possible answers. If nothing else, writing down your possible answers gets that obsession out of your head. You don't need to agonize for days about what you wish you had said.

What questions drives you nuts?

Questions that I hate:

_____

_____

_____

_____

* * *

Asking for the job
Before the interview ends, ask for the job. Its okay, you're allowed to ask for what you want.

Start by asking about their objections. Ask "are there any concerns that would keep you from hiring me?" And of course, you will need to answer those objections. Be honest and forthright; don't fall into tap dancing at this point.

Don't forget to ask about their process. "When do you expect to make a decision?" "Do you have more candidates to interview?" These are very legitimate questions at any interview. Asking questions along this line shows your interest in the job.

Your manner should show your enthusiasm for the job (even if you don't want it.) You can always turn down an offer for an unacceptable situation, but if you get in the habit of playing the interview game to win, you will have the luxury of choosing to say "no" or "yes."

Close with a strong statement about your desires. "I've really enjoyed learning more about your company, and would love to work with you," is a wonderful, simple statement. You don't need to say anything more. In fact, practice this line with friends and family before your interview to get accustomed to being bold.

Leaving with grace
After your final pitch, it's time to get out of there. Thank everyone for their time and get business cards. Be sure to leave them with one of yours. You can ask when you should follow up with them, but don't press the issue at this point. Goodbyes are a formal process, filled with formalities. Be nice and don't drag it out. Some of the best impressions involve a tactful exit.

Thank you notes
Thank you notes are essential. Believe it or not, but many candidates fail to send this important professional courtesy. Sincerely thanking the interviewer will set you apart. Send thank you notes for both phone and in-person interviews.

Your first thank you note should be in the same media as your initial contact. If you have communicated through email, send it that way. If you began the relationship through LinkedIn, send a note from there. If you didn't have direct contact with the hiring manager before meeting, use their email address from their business card.

Thank you notes need to be sent quickly. Send your electronic thanks as soon as you get back to your computer. However, don't stop there. Use traditional thank you cards as well - yes, hand-written, snail mail thank you cards. When they receive your card in the mail several days later, it will remind them of you.

Content is important. You cannot introduce new material in your thank you note. This is not an opportunity to mention anything that you forgot in the interview. Nor is this a chance for you to answer a question "correctly." If you really blew a question, don't remind the interviewer of your mistake.

In your thank you note, point out two or three strong points that were discussed in the interview. Remind them of your examples. Write about your enthusiasm for the job and the company. If you did really connect with the interviewer, mention the points where you felt in sync. It may even be something not related about the job, such as a commonality from your introduction. You want them to remember you as a person. In your conclusion, stress that you look forward to hearing from them again.

* * *

Final words on interviewing
A successful interview will not only leave the interviewer with a positive impression of you, but gives you information about the company as well. Finding a job is about getting the right fit on both sides of the table. When you remember that you have a choice about your next job, you are empowered.

If you get nervous or shy about the whole interview process, practice with someone. Don't just lob friendly questions at each other. Try using the different interview styles. Make sure they use the hated interview questions as well. Dress for the mock interview; do everything as real as possible to test your own abilities. Even better, practice with a group. Using others as an audience teaches you how to manage your nerves, and they can provide feedback as well. Taping yourself during a mock interview can reveal a lot about your own body language and appearance.

One manager I knew preferred to hire people who got nervous during the job interview. In his mind, this showed that the candidate cared about the job. It is true that nervous and introverted people get hired every day. Prepare yourself, take a deep breath, and mind your manners. You will do just fine.

Chapter 12 - Tips to Maintain Your Sanity

Job searching seems like the worst job in the world. It's lonely being stuck at home, flipping through online ads and company websites. There is very little feedback from employers. Most can't be bothered to even send a rejection letter. It's demoralizing, stressful, discouraging and boring all at the same time.

Plus, your boss - yourself - is constantly nagging in your head, undermining your efforts with doubt and impatience. As the time between jobs lengthens, so does the accompanying depression and fear. "What if I don't find a job soon enough? What if I don't find something that will pay me what I'm worth? Maybe I don't deserve that much anyway... Maybe I can't find a job because there is something wrong with me..." The inner critic is ready to jump at any fault or problem, both real and imagined. However, these negative attitudes only have power when we feed into them.

Keep the faith

It's important to keep the faith - belief in yourself, belief in the job market and belief that the right job is out there, waiting for you.

Consider this: every bit of research is educating you, opening your mind to new possibilities for that perfect job. Every job you apply for hones your tactics and your materials. Every interview is grooming you, allowing you to be polished, professional and natural when the right job emerges. Do not be discouraged by negative feedback; the universe is training you to ensure your future success.

In times of doubt, look for the subtle reminders all around you. Gratitude for what you do have instead of bitterness about what you lost is pure magic. A grateful heart knows peace and serenity, which translates to confidence and a positive attitude. What benefits have you gained through your job search? Maybe you found an old friend through LinkedIn. Maybe it is extra time to reconnect with your family and friends. It can even be a break from a highly stressful job. Time in between jobs gives you the opportunity to sort through your feelings about your employment change before joining a new work environment. Sometimes you have to heal before you can move on.

Giving back rejuvenates the spirit. Stretch beyond your confines of the house and volunteer in your community, gaining new contacts and helping others at the same time.

When faith looks thin, walk away from your computer. Desperately searching through endless websites will not yield positive results. It adds to the gray haze in your mind, leading to dismal outlooks for your future. Take a break, both physically and mentally. Go for a walk or a drive. Changing your scenery makes it easier to change your outlook. The world won't collapse because you took a mental health moment.

Come back with fresh eyes and pick a different task. Don't keep beating yourself against the metaphorical wall, thinking that sheer force will break through.

If what you are doing is not yielding real results, try new ideas and new tactics. After all, one definition of insanity is doing the same thing over and over, while expecting different results. Save yourself from this problem and try something new.

Benchmarks to Guide your success

How do you know if your job search is effective? For most people, they say, "When I get an interview or job offer." However, that does nothing to determine your success while you are early in the job search.

Like any goal-driven activity, it is important to know the benchmarks along the way to track your progress. Most people don't know critical numbers in relation to their job search.

To see how your efforts compare, look at these common factors:

1. How long does a job search take?
    o   For every $10,000 of salary, add one month to your search
        A $40,000 job takes 4 months to land, but an executive of $100,000 can take up to 10 months. Maximum for most top executives can reach one year. However, learning more about the hiring process can significantly minimize this time. In addition to the suggestions in this book, taking a job search class or using a consultant can add new tools to your arsenal and speed up the process.

240

2. <u>How many resumes do I have to send before I get an interview?</u>
   o 10 to 20 if you carefully research most of the jobs
   o 20 to 50 in a cool market
   o 100+ if you are not doing any research
   If you have sent over 30 resumes without a single phone interview, you need to re-evaluate your resume and/or your tactics. This may include an analysis of your chosen industry.

3. <u>How long does it take to get a response about a job?</u>
   o Most job postings are open for 1 to 2 weeks. It takes another 1-2 weeks for HR to make their recommendations. Phone interviews are scheduled 3-4 weeks after a job posts.
   o Highly technical, executive level or niche market openings have a longer hiring cycle. Expect phone interviews within 45-60 days.
   o Government jobs may take up to 3 months to schedule interviews.
   Since HR departments can have a long screening process, it is essential to send a resume directly to the hiring manager as well as following HR's procedures.

4. <u>How many jobs should I apply to each week?</u>
   o 10 if you research every position
   o 10-30 if you send out stock cover letters/ resumes or applying to blind ads through an employment website
   It is better to apply to a few, well-researched positions than to rely on submitting to several blind ads you saw posted on the major employment sites. However, you do not want to overlook any opportunity.

5. <u>How much time do I have to apply for a job?</u>
   o If there is no deadline published, plan on the job being open for 3-5 business days.
   o Smaller businesses will close their jobs faster
   Some companies are required to keep a job open for a set period of time. In that case, as long as it is before the deadline, you can apply at any time.

Small and medium sized businesses are known to keep a job open until they feel that they received a significant applicant pool. For this, this can be as short as 1-3 days.

6. How much should I spend on my job search?
   o 1% to 3% of your target salary
   You need to invest in your job search. Expenses can include professional resume services, books, classes, professional pictures, clothing, employment website fees, parking and so on. Depending on your industry and experience level, expect to pay from $250 to $900 for a professionally written resume.
   You do not have to pay a recruiter a placement fee, which ranges between 10-30% of your annual salary. Employers should pay placement fees.

7. How much time does it take to write a good resume?
   o A professional can create a comprehensive resume in 4-5 hours.
   o If you are writing your own resume, wait a day before sending it out. Use this time to get other people to review it.
   o Online and interactive resumes will take longer, depending on the additional elements added.
   o A targeted cover letter can take up to an hour or more to draft.
   Slamming a resume out quickly just to get it done will not be effective. Take the time to research the universal criteria for your desired job, not just what you think is important. Same with cover letters: consider the employers' needs, and write about how you can answer it.

8. How many hours a week should I spend on my job search?
   o 20-40 hours a week
   Once your tools are in place - online profiles built, resumes written, cover letters drafted - devote more time to networking and research.

Job searching is a tough business. Accept the fact that it will take some time, effort, patience and money. While the silence may be maddening, keep track of the amount of resumes you send and compare it with your results. You may uncover problems with your tactics. In sales, it is well known that only 5% of your initial contacts will lead to an opportunity. Keep in mind that every "no" gets you closer to the "yes."

* * *

Answers to common frustrations
Maintaining your sanity requires managing your frustrations. Looking for a job is not easy, and unchecked frustrations only add to the anxiety levels. By now, you've already developed some of your own pet peeves about the hiring process, wondering why they would treat candidates this way. Do any of these sound familiar?

1. Why won't they send a rejection letter? I just want to know either way...
   - It's cheap to be rude. HR is swamped with hundreds of resumes. Rejection letters are the very bottom of their priority list. Even an automated reply requires updating the database. To help get around this time-consuming tasks, many companies now use an automated response when you apply to the job, which includes statements like "We will contact you if your skills and experience is appropriate for the position." If you don't hear back from a company within 4-6 weeks, it's safe to assume you didn't make the cut.

2. If a job closes in two weeks, why do they leave the ad on an employment site for two months?
   - HR departments get so busy that they forget to take the job down OR...
   - They want to keep the field open. If the top candidates fall through, it costs money to re-list the job opening. However, keeping the same posting up costs no extra cash.

3. I interviewed but didn't get the job. When I asked for feedback as to why, I only got vague and generalized answers. Why?
   - Legal reasons. No company wants to open this can of worms. Hiring decisions are confidential, especially in the legal-happy attitudes of the American public. If you are

working with a professional recruiter, you might get better feedback. However, even this answer will be guarded. This is another reason why it is helpful to work with a job search counselor to gain professional advice and critiques.

4. <u>How can I research blind ads to get directly to the hiring manager?</u>
   - You can't - that's why they ran a blind ad. However, if you are in touch with your industry and staying on top of the news, you might be able to make an educated guess.
   - If you can't deduce the company, submit your best cover letter and resume for the situation. While you can't discuss their specific business, use some tricks from this book to stand out from the crowd.

5. <u>Two separate experts reviewed my resume and gave me vastly different opinions. Which one should I believe?</u>
   - Consider the source. Do they understand your field? Are they looking at the content, or just the format? What is their expertise? All resume reviews are subjective, but for accurate advice, ask someone who understands *the hiring manager's point-f-view,* not just stock answers or cheeky marketing tactics.

6. <u>I got strong feedback from the interviewers that I had the job, but the company decided to not hire anyone. Why go through the motions?</u>
   - Their priorities changed, which probably had nothing to do with you. However, if you can convince the potential employer that you will save the company money or make money (or both), the hiring manager or HR person is more likely to champion your cause.

7. <u>Competition is too tough - too many people are looking for work.</u>
   - Competition is a good thing. It demands that you do your best work. Plus, over 90% of the candidates are going to bomb in the screening process; 75% won't even make it to the third round. Learn from their errors, you won't be making those mistakes.

8. I've been looking so long, I feel like I will never get hired.
   Employers aren't interested in me because I am (*pick one or all*)
   too old, overqualified, under qualified, been out of work too long,
   etc. etc.

   - If you start buying into these preconceived notions, that is
     all that you will find. Just as we addressed the employer's
     objections in "Dealing with Discrepancies," you need to
     answer your own objections. What old negative thought
     patterns are holding you back?

It is important to acknowledge your frustrations, but don't let
them consume you. Focusing on the negative makes it very difficult to
affect positive change in your life. Your job search should be a chance
to move forward or in a new direction. To do that, you need to let go
of the pain.

* * *

Managing your Motivation and Mentality
Part of conducting a healthy job search is recognizing your personal
barriers, blocks and boundaries...

Shiny things and other distractions
You will probably have lapses in your discipline. Giving in to
distractions every now and then is normal human behavior. However,
look out if every tiny thing that comes along distracts you from the
task at hand. Don't let daytime TV suck away hours of your time with
no positive benefit.

If you find yourself wandering around your house every 30
minutes, ask yourself why. Is the job search getting too frustrating?
Are you avoiding doing the research necessary to find the jobs? Are
you discouraged about the lack of open positions?

Is there an undercurrent of fear in your job search? Lack of
motivation in your hunt can be a warning sign of subconscious
avoidance. Procrastination is another red flag. Rather than subjecting
yourself to more rejection, you start letting distractions divert you
from the task at hand.

When the shiny things become overwhelming, do some journal writing. Take 10 minutes and ask yourself "What am I afraid of?" Be honest – then write down a solution to that fear. Fear of rejection is one of the main stumbling blocks. Keep in mind that every "no" brings you closer to the "yes."

Then there is the biggest distraction of all - your own computer. I can't tell you how many times I sit down to get to check my email and get sucked into reading the celebrity gossip online for an hour. Or playing with my virtual pets on Facebook. Or instant messaging my husband - okay, he's the one who starts that, but I have to answer, right? Just what is going on here? For most of us, the computer is our playground as well as our workspace. Just imagine trying to teach 2nd graders math while they are on the jungle gym... chaos, right? The same thing happens when our desire to play clashes with our need to work.

To help manage the playground aspect, set aside specific time to catch up on the fun stuff. It is important to take these mental breaks. For me, I limit my virtual pets to the first 10-15 minutes of my day. This way, I don't feel guilty when I play, nor do I feel resentful because I didn't get to relax. Give your inner child recess and your work will be more effective.

Desperation

Your worst enemy is desperation. As the months wear on, despair settles in, accompanied by her big sister desperation. Desperation causes you to throw away your standards. Desperation makes you blind to the red flags of intolerable situations. Desperation can creep into your voice during interviews. Desperation leads to bad decisions.

Next thing you know, you apply to jobs that you would never have considered before. An internal dialogue convinces you that you could be successful in a high-commission sales job, or that you would be happy doing the administrative assistant job far below your experience. You persuade yourself that an hour-long commute gives you the "alone time" you need. The inner voice assures you that abandoning your chosen field is the only course of action.

Are you really sincere about these career options? Or is it desperation that turns your head from your goals?

Check your motives. Making a career change is not a bad thing, but a desperate move won't be successful. Two horrible things can happen: you can either get the job or not. If you accept a job far below your capabilities, this brings even more personal questioning of your worth. On the other side, not gaining an interview is demoralizing, especially after you dropped your standards. It is demoralizing to receive nothing but rejections, especially with a dumbed-down resume.

There is nothing wrong with taking a lower position, but it needs to be a constructive change, not a desperate one. Your resume and cover letter require a specific tactic to get a response from the employers. To convey the right message, you need to believe it first.

Write your new employment goals in an encouraging manner. Accept the change mentally before reaching out to employers. Acceptance of change leads to developing a positive attitude. In the hiring game, attitude makes the difference between a job offer and a rejection letter.

Get out of the house and give back
The best way to break out of your mental prison is to do something for somebody else. It can be formal volunteer work with a non-profit company, or it can be helping a friend with his garden. It doesn't matter what it is, so long as you get physically moving and interacting with others. Don't treat this as networking, although that might be a side effect. The idea is to do something without selfish motives.

Believe it or not, nothing will protect your sanity better than giving back to your world.

Networking, Support and Social Groups
Job searching support groups can be a help or a hindrance, depending on the outlook of the group members. Listen to the tone of the group; are they encouraging and hopeful, or is it a hotbed of discontent? Don't stay with a group that engages in negative behaviors, such as sarcasm, biting remarks or outright attacks of others don't stay. Job searching is hard enough without listening to others' negative outlook.

A healthy networking group will do more than share job leads. They encourage each other, share industry news and provide honest feedback. Some groups bring in guest speakers or experts. Some others may coordinate social activities or organize volunteer efforts.

Don't overlook groups that provide support. This can be a formal support group managed by a mental health facility, or a casual get-together of job seekers who want to address all of the issues brought about with job searching. Support groups allow people to talk about their real concerns in a safe environment. If you have this safety valve, you will be more likely to speak positively in an interview.

Another key is to join groups just for fun and socialization. The social website www.meetup.com has literally thousands of groups in your area that meet every week. The whole point is to get together with other people that share a common interest. It is free to join, although some groups charge for their specific activities. What's great is that every interest has its own group - from Star Wars fans to hiking enthusiasts, it is a great way to invigorate your spirit by expanding your horizons.

Keep fun alive
Just because you are looking for work doesn't mean that it is the only thing you do. Set aside time to cut loose. You don't need to spend a lot of money either; in fact, discovering free activities in your town can be part of the fun. Check out community events and free days at your local museum or zoo. Many cities sponsor free community events year-round. Explore local hiking trails and parks. Even the tourist attractions can give you a new appreciation of your hometown.

Make the most of what you already have. Dust off your board games and invite friends over. If you don't watch your DVDs, sell them on eBay to go buy some more. Used bookstores usually let you trade in books for store credit as well. Game Stop and Game Crazy do the same thing for video games.

Think about saving money wherever you go. Clipping coupons can make a big difference. Many restaurants and businesses run coupons all the time. A quick website search will reveal deals, either through their own website or through the coupon outlets. Google the business name and "coupons" to reveal great options. And of course, daily deals websites like Groupon.com and LivingSocial.com offer 50% off from tons of restaurants and businesses.

Appreciate the abundance around you every day. The good things in life will always be found when they are sought.

* * *

Final words on sanity

Your job search is a temporary phase in your life. Done correctly, it can reveal more to you than just a new income source. Job searching can teach you balance, a lesson you can continue in your professional like.

For your own mental health, watch your motives. Are you driven by hope and faith or fear and desperation? Write about it in a private journal; recognizing your feelings in an avenue separate from your job search will keep the doubts out of your professional communications. Throughout your job search, you have the ability to affect your attitude. Believe that you are valuable, talented and effective. When you believe it, the employers will too.

Conclusion - It Can Happen

In the quiet of your house, you carefully review your notes about your top target companies. You have them narrowed down to your top three choices. You made contact with one of the CEOs through a common LinkedIn group, and managed to send him your resume. You are hopeful, but still keeping your options open.

The phone rings. Caller ID shows an unfamiliar number, but it is the company's name that makes you gasp. It's your top choice! Your pulse quickens as you answer the phone in a professional manner. Your voice does not waiver or betray your anticipation. It is the HR department,

"Our CEO asked me to call you and find out why you are so interested in our company," the screener asks. "Do you have a moment to answer some questions?"

You agree. You are prepared, confident and relaxed. You recognize her screening questions. The line of conversation confirms what you believed to be the top qualifications for the job. She is impressed, and schedules you to come in the following week.

The office is refined and elegant, but everyone is friendly and personable. The receptionist is glad to answer your questions about the company, especially since you show interest in her and her job. The company lists their charitable donations on the wall of the lobby; you notice one where you volunteer. You decide to use a friendly introduction that mentions your common support of the charity.

The CEO's executive assistant leads you to the conference room where you meet with her and the HR screener. Their styles are different, but you are not rattled by the combined skepticism and conflicting openness. You secretly give thanks that you brought several copies of your resume, as they look over your experience once again.

Your answers are clear and confident. Your questions are insightful and relevant. The pair is proud to introduce you to the CEO. Within moments, your rapport is established by your common enthusiasm for the arts - an interest that you already knew from his LinkedIn profile. The conversation is professional and results-driven.

Your skills fit their needs exactly, and you well practiced in presenting them during the interview.

Now it is only a matter of the formalities to get you on board with your dream job.

* * *

Did you enjoy that? Good. Because this future can be a reality for you. Keep the faith - it can happen!

Made in the USA
San Bernardino, CA
24 December 2016